# VIRGINIBUS PUERISQUE

## AND OTHER PAPERS

## WORKS BY ROBERT LOUIS STEVENSON

AN INLAND VOYAGE.
EDINBURGH: PICTURESQUE NOTES.
TRAVELS WITH A DONKEY.
VIRGINIBUS PUERISQUE.
FAMILIAR STUDIES OF MEN AND BOOKS.
NEW ARABIAN NIGHTS.
TREASURE ISLAND.
THE SILVERADO SQUATTERS.
A CHILD'S GARDEN OF VERSES.
PRINCE OTTO.
THE STRANGE CASE OF DR. JEKYLL AND MR. HYDE.
KIDNAPPED.
THE MERRY MEN.
UNDERWOODS.
MEMORIES AND PORTRAITS.
THE BLACK ARROW.
THE MASTER OF BALLANTRAE.
FATHER DAMIEN: AN OPEN LETTER.
BALLADS.
ACROSS THE PLAINS.
ISLAND NIGHTS ENTERTAINMENTS.
A FOOTNOTE TO HISTORY.
CATRIONA.
WEIR OF HERMISTON.
VAILIMA LETTERS.
LETTERS TO HIS FAMILY AND FRIENDS.
FABLES.
SONGS OF TRAVEL.
ST. IVES.
IN THE SOUTH SEAS.
ESSAYS OF TRAVEL.
TALES AND FANTASIES.
THE ART OF WRITING.
LAY MORALS, ETC.
RECORDS OF A FAMILY OF ENGINEERS.
MEMOIR OF FLEMING JENKIN.
PRAYERS WRITTEN AT VAILIMA.
THE WAIF WOMAN.
ON THE CHOICE OF A PROFESSION.
NEW POEMS.

### WITH MRS. STEVENSON

THE DYNAMITER.

### WITH LLOYD OSBOURNE

THE WRONG BOX. THE WRECKER. THE EBB-TIDE.

# VIRGINIBUS PUERISQUE

## AND OTHER PAPERS

BY

ROBERT LOUIS STEVENSON

LONDON
CHATTO & WINDUS
1919

*Printed at* THE BALLANTYNE PRESS
SPOTTISWOODE, BALLANTYNE & CO. LTD.
*Colchester, London & Eton, England*

My dear William Ernest Henley,

We are all busy in this world building Towers of Babel; and the child of our imaginations is always a changeling when it comes from nurse. This is not only true in the greatest, as of wars and folios, but in the least also, like the trifling volume in your hand. Thus I began to write these papers with a definite end: I was to be the *Advocatus*, not I hope *Diaboli*, but *Juventutis;* I was to state temperately the beliefs of youth as opposed to the contentions of age; to go over all the field where the two differ, and produce at last a little volume of special pleadings which I might call, without misnomer, *Life at Twenty-five.* But times kept changing, and I shared in the change. I clung hard to that entrancing age; but, with the best will, no man can be twenty-five for ever. The old, ruddy convictions deserted me, and, along with them, the style that fits their presentation and defence. I saw, and indeed my friends informed me, that the game was up. A good part of the volume would answer to the long-projected title; but the shadows of the prison-house are on the rest.

It is good to have been young in youth and, as years go on, to grow older. Many are already old before they are through their teens; but to travel deliberately through one's ages is to get the heart out of a liberal education. Times change, opinions vary to their opposite, and still this world appears a brave gymnasium, full of sea-bathing, and horse exercise, and bracing, manly virtues; and what can be more encouraging than to find the friend who was welcome at one age, still welcome at another? Our affections and beliefs are wiser than we; the best that is in us is better than we can understand; for it is grounded beyond experience, and guides us, blindfold but safe, from one age on to another.

These papers are like milestones on the wayside of my life; and as I look back in memory, there is hardly a stage of that distance but I see you present with advice, reproof, or praise. Meanwhile, many things have changed, you and I among the rest: but I hope that our sympathy, founded on the love of our art, and nourished by mutual assistance, shall survive these little revolutions undiminished, and, with God's help, unite us to the end.

R. L. S.

DAVOS PLATZ, 1881.

# CONTENTS

# "VIRGINIBUS PUERISQUE"

# "VIRGINIBUS PUERISQUE"

## I

WITH the single exception of Falstaff, all Shakespeare's characters are what we call marrying men. Mercutio, as he was own cousin to Benedick and Biron, would have come to the same end in the long run. Even Iago had a wife, and, what is far stranger, he was jealous. People like Jacques and the Fool in *Lear*, although we can hardly imagine they would ever marry, kept single out of a cynical humour or for a broken heart, and not, as we do nowadays, from a spirit of incredulity and preference for the single state. For that matter, if you turn to George Sand's French version of *As You Like It* (and I think I can promise you will like it but little), you will find Jacques marries Celia just as Orlando marries Rosalind.

At least there seems to have been much less hesitation over marriage in Shakespeare's days; and what hesitation there was was of a laughing sort, and not much more serious, one way or the other, than that of Panurge. In modern comedies the heroes are mostly of Benedick's way of thinking, but twice as much in earnest, and not one quarter so confident. And I take this diffidence as a proof of how sincere their terror is. They know they are only human after all; they know what gins and pitfalls lie about their feet; and how the shadow of matrimony waits, resolute and awful, at the cross-roads. They would wish to keep their liberty; but if that may not be, why, God's will be done! "What, are you afraid of marriage?" asks Cécile, in *Maître Guerin.* "Oh, mon Dieu, non!" replies Arthur; "I should take chloroform." They look forward to marriage much in the same way as they prepare themselves for death: each seems inevitable; each is a great Perhaps, and a leap into the dark, for which, when a man is in the blue devils, he has specially to harden his heart. That splendid scoundrel, Maxime de Trailles, took the news of marriages much as an old man hears the deaths of his contemporaries. "C'est désespérant," he cried, throwing himself down in the arm-chair at Madame Schontz's; "c'est désespérant, nous nous marions tous!" Every marriage was like another gray hair on his head; and the jolly church bells seemed to taunt him with his fifty years and fair round belly.

The fact is, we are much more afraid of life than our ancestors, and cannot find it in our hearts either to marry or not to marry. Marriage is terrifying, but so is a cold and forlorn old age. The friendships of men are vastly agreeable, but they are insecure. You know all the time that one friend will marry and put you to the door; a second accept a situation in China, and become no more to you than a name, a reminiscence, and an occasional crossed letter, very laborious to read; a third will take up with some religious crotchet and treat you to sour looks thenceforward. So, in one way or another, life forces men apart and breaks up the goodly fellowships for ever. The very flexibility and ease which make men's friendships so agreeable while they endure, make them the easier to destroy and forget. And a man who has a few friends, or one who has a dozen (if there be any one so wealthy on this earth), cannot forget on how precarious a base his happiness reposes; and how by a stroke or two of fate—a death, a few light words, a piece of stamped paper, a woman's bright eyes—he may be left, in a month, destitute of all. Marriage is certainly a perilous remedy. Instead of on two or three, you stake your happiness on one life only. But still, as the bargain is more explicit and complete on your part, it is more so on the other; and you have not to fear so many contingencies; it is not every wind that can blow you from your anchorage; and so long as Death withholds his sickle, you will always have a friend at home. People who share a cell in the Bastile, or are thrown together on an uninhabited isle, if they do not immediately fall to fisticuffs, will find some possible ground of compromise. They will learn each other's ways and humours, so as to know where they must go warily, and where they may lean their whole weight. The discretion of the first years becomes the settled habit of the last; and so, with wisdom and patience, two lives may grow indissolubly into one.

But marriage, if comfortable, is not at all heroic. It certainly narrows and damps the spirits of generous men. In marriage, a man becomes slack and selfish, and undergoes a fatty degeneration of his moral being. It is not only when Lydgate misallies himself with Rosamond Vincy, but when Ladislaw marries above him with Dorothea, that this may be exemplified. The air of the fireside withers out all the fine wildings of the husband's heart. He is so comfortable and happy that he begins to prefer comfort and happiness to everything else on earth, his wife included. Yesterday he would have shared his last shilling; to-day "his first duty is to his family," and is fulfilled in large measure by laying down vintages and husbanding the health of an invaluable parent. Twenty years ago this man was equally capable of crime or heroism; now he is fit for neither. His soul is asleep, and you may speak without constraint; you will not wake him. It is not for nothing that Don Quixote was a bachelor and Marcus Aurelius married ill. For women, there is less of this danger. Marriage is of so much use to a woman, opens out to her so much more of life, and puts her in the way of so much more freedom and usefulness, that, whether she marry ill or well, she can hardly miss some benefit. It is true, however, that some of the merriest and most genuine of women are old maids; and that those old maids, and wives who are unhappily married, have often most of the true motherly touch. And this would seem to show, even for women, some narrowing influence in comfortable married life. But the rule is none the less certain: if you wish the pick of men and women, take a good bachelor and a good wife.

I am often filled with wonder that so many marriages are passably successful, and so few come to open failure, the more so as I fail to understand the principle on which people regulate their choice. I see women marrying indiscriminately with staring burgesses and ferret-faced, white-eyed boys, and men dwell in contentment with noisy scullions, or taking into their lives acidulous vestals. It is a common answer to say the good people marry because they fall in love; and of course you may use and misuse a word as much as you please, if you have the world along with you. But love is at least a somewhat hyperbolical expression for such lukewarm preference. It is not here, anyway, that Love employs his golden shafts; he cannot be said, with any fitness of language, to reign here and revel. Indeed, if this be love at all, it is plain the poets have been fooling with mankind since the foundation of the world. And you have only to look these happy couples in the face, to see they have never been in love, or in hate, or in any other high passion all their days. When you see a dish of fruit at dessert, you sometimes set your affections upon one particular peach or nectarine, watch it with some anxiety as it comes round the table, and feel quite a sensible disappointment when it is taken by some one else. I have used the phrase "high passion." Well, I should say this was about as high a passion as generally leads to marriage. One husband hears after marriage that some poor fellow is dying of his wife's love. "What a pity!" he exclaims; "you know I could so easily have got another!" And yet that is a very happy union. Or again: A young man was telling me the sweet story of his loves. "I like it well enough as long as her sisters are there," said this amorous swain; "but I don't know what to do when we're alone." Once more: A married lady was debating the subject with another lady. "You know, dear," said the first, "after ten years of marriage, if he is nothing else, your husband is always an old friend." "I have many old friends," returned the other, "but I prefer them to be nothing more." "Oh, perhaps I might *prefer* that also!" There is a common note in these three illustrations of the modern idyll; and it must be owned the god goes among us with a limping gait and blear eyes. You wonder whether it was so always; whether desire was always equally dull and spiritless, and possession equally cold. I cannot help fancying most people make, ere they marry, some such table of recommendations as Hannah Godwin wrote to her brother William anent her friend, Miss Gay. It is so charmingly comical, and so pat to the occasion, that I must quote a few phrases. "The young lady is in every sense formed to make one of your disposition really happy. She has a pleasing voice, with which she accompanies her musical instrument with judgment. She has an easy politeness in her manners, neither free nor reserved. She is a good housekeeper and a good economist, and yet of a generous disposition. As to her internal accomplishments, I have reason to speak still more highly of them: good sense without vanity, a penetrating judgment without a disposition to satire, with about as much religion as my William likes, struck me with a wish that she was my William's wife." That is about the tune: pleasing voice, moderate good looks, unimpeachable internal accomplishments after the style of the copy-book, with about as much religion as my William likes; and then, with all speed, to church.

To deal plainly, if they only married when they fell in love, most people would die unwed; and among the others, there would be not a few tumultuous households. The Lion is the King of Beasts, but he is scarcely suitable for a domestic pet. In the same way, I suspect love is rather too violent a passion to make, in all cases, a good domestic sentiment. Like other violent excitements, it throws up not only what is best, but what is worst and smallest, in men's characters. Just as some people are malicious in drink, or brawling and virulent under the influence of religious feeling, some are moody, jealous, and exacting when they are in love, who are honest, downright, good-hearted fellows enough in the everyday affairs and humours of the world.

How then, seeing we are driven to the hypothesis that people choose in comparatively cold blood, how is it they choose so well? One is almost tempted to hint that it does not much matter whom you marry; that, in fact, marriage is a subjective affection, and if you have made up your mind to it, and once talked yourself fairly over, you could "pull it through" with anybody. But even if we take matrimony at its lowest, even if we regard it as no more than a sort of friendship recognised by the police, there must be degrees in the freedom and sympathy realised, and some principle to guide simple folk in their selection. Now what should this principle be? Are there no more definite rules than are to be found in the Prayer-book? Law and religion forbid the banns on the ground of propinquity or consanguinity; society steps in to separate classes; and in all this most critical matter, has common sense, has wisdom, never a word to say? In the absence of more magisterial teaching, let us talk it over between friends: even a few guesses may be of interest to youths and maidens.

In all that concerns eating and drinking, company, climate, and ways of life, community of taste is to be sought for. It would be trying, for instance, to keep bed and board with an early riser or a vegetarian. In matters of art and intellect, I believe it is of no consequence. Certainly it is of none in the companionships of men, who will dine more readily with one who has a good heart, a good cellar, and a humorous tongue, than with another who shares all their favourite hobbies and is melancholy withal. If your wife likes Tupper, that is no reason why you should hang your head. She thinks with the majority, and has the courage of her opinions. I have always suspected public taste to be a mongrel product, out of affectation by dogmatism; and felt sure, if you could only find an honest man of no special literary bent, he would tell you he thought much of Shakespeare bombastic and most absurd, and all of him written in very obscure English and wearisome to read. And not long ago I was able to lay by my lantern in content, for I found the honest man. He was a fellow of parts, quick, humorous, a clever painter, and with an eye for certain poetical effects of sea and ships. I am not much of a judge of that kind of thing, but a sketch of his comes before me sometimes at night. How strong, supple, and living the ship seems upon the billows! With what a dip and rake she shears the flying sea! I cannot fancy the man who saw this effect, and took it on the wing with so much force and spirit, was what you call commonplace in the last recesses of the heart. And yet he thought, and was not ashamed to have it known of him, that Ouida was better in every way than William Shakespeare. If there were more people of his honesty, this would be about the staple of lay criticism. It is not taste that is plentiful, but courage that is rare. And what have we in place? How many, who think no otherwise than the young painter, have we not heard disbursing second-hand hyperboles? Have you never turned sick at heart, O best of critics! when some of your own sweet adjectives were returned on you before a gaping audience? Enthusiasm about art is become a function of the average female being, which she performs with precision and a sort of haunting sprightliness, like an ingenious and well-regulated machine. Sometimes, alas! the calmest man is carried away in the torrent, bandies adjectives with the best, and out-Herods Herod for some shameful moments. When you remember that, you will be tempted to put things strongly, and say you will marry no one who is not like George the Second, and cannot state openly a distaste for poetry and painting.

The word "facts" is, in some ways, crucial. I have spoken with Jesuits and Plymouth Brethren, mathematicians and poets, dogmatic republicans and dear old gentlemen in bird's-eye neckcloths; and each understood the word "facts" in an occult sense of his own. Try as I might, I could get no nearer the principle of their division. What was essential to them, seemed to me trivial or untrue. We could come to no compromise as to what was, or what was not, important in the life of man. Turn as we pleased, we all stood back to back in a big ring, and saw another quarter of the heavens, with different mountain-tops along the sky-line and different constellations overhead. We had each of us some whimsy in the brain, which we believed more than anything else, and which discoloured all experience to its own shade. How would you have people agree, when one is deaf and the other blind? Now this is where there should be community between man and wife. They should be agreed on their catchword in "*facts of religion*," or "*facts of science*," or "*society, my dear*"; for without such an agreement all intercourse is a painful strain upon the mind. "About as much religion as my William likes," in short, that is what is necessary to make a happy couple of any William and his spouse. For there are differences which no habit nor affection can reconcile, and the Bohemian must not intermarry with the Pharisee. Imagine Consuelo as Mrs. Samuel Budget, the wife of the successful merchant!

The best of men and the best of women may sometimes live together all their lives, and, for want of some consent on fundamental questions, hold each other lost spirits to the end.

A certain sort of talent is almost indispensable for people who would spend years together and not bore themselves to death. But the talent, like the agreement, must be for and about life. To dwell happily together, they should be versed in the niceties of the heart, and born with a faculty for willing compromise. The woman must be talented as a woman, and it will not much matter although she is talented in nothing else. She must know her *métier de femme,* and have a fine touch for the affections. And it is more important that a person should be a good gossip, and talk pleasantly and smartly of common friends and the thousand and one nothings of the day and hour, than that she should speak with the tongues of men and angels; for a while together by the fire, happens more frequently in marriage than the presence of a distinguished foreigner to dinner. That people should laugh over the same sort of jests, and have many a story of "grouse in the gun-room," many an old joke between them which time cannot wither nor custom stale, is a better preparation for life, by your leave, than many other things higher and better sounding in the world's ears. You could read Kant by yourself, if you wanted; but you must share a joke with some one else. You can forgive people who do not follow you through a philosophical disquisition; but to find your wife laughing when you had tears in your eyes, or staring when you were in a fit of laughter, would go some way towards a dissolution of the marriage.

I know a woman who, from some distaste or disability,

could never so much as understand the meaning of the word *politics*, and has given up trying to distinguish Whigs from Tories; but take her on her own politics, ask her about other men or women and the chicanery of everyday existence—the rubs, the tricks, the vanities on which life turns—and you will not find many more shrewd, trenchant, and humorous. Nay, to make plainer what I have in mind, this same woman has a share of the higher and more poetical understanding, frank interest in things for their own sake, and enduring astonishment at the most common. She is not to be deceived by custom, or made to think a mystery solved when it is repeated. I have heard her say she could wonder herself crazy over the human eyebrow. Now in a world where most of us walk very contentedly in the little lit circle of their own reason, and have to be reminded of what lies without by specious and clamant exceptions—earthquakes, eruptions of Vesuvius, banjos floating in mid-air at a *séance*, and the like—a mind so fresh and unsophisticated is no despicable gift. I will own I think it a better sort of mind than goes necessarily with the clearest views on public business. It will wash. It will find something to say at an odd moment. It has in it the spring of pleasant and quaint fancies. Whereas I can imagine myself yawning all night long until my jaws ached and the tears came into my eyes, although my companion on the other side of the hearth held the most enlightened opinions on the franchise or the ballot.

The question of professions, in as far as they regard marriage, was only interesting to women until of late days, but it touches all of us now. Certainly, if I could help it, I would never marry a wife who wrote. The practice of letters is miserably harassing to the mind; and after an hour or two's work, all the more human portion of the author is extinct; he will bully, backbite, and speak daggers. Music, I hear, is not much better. But painting, on the contrary, is often highly sedative; because so much of the labour, after your picture is once begun, is almost entirely manual, and of that skilled sort of manual labour which offers a continual series of successes, and so tickles a man, through his vanity, into good humour. Alas! in letters there is nothing of this sort. You may write as beautiful a hand as you will, you have always something else to think of, and cannot pause to notice your loops and flourishes; they are beside the mark, and the first law stationer could put you to the blush. Rousseau, indeed, made some account of penmanship, even made it a source of livelihood, when he copied out the *Héloïse* for *dilettante* ladies; and therein showed that strange eccentric prudence which guided him among so many thousand follies and insanities. It would be well for all of the *genus irritabile* thus to add something of skilled labour to intangible brain-work. To find the right word is so doubtful a success and lies so near to failure, that there is no satisfaction in a year of it; but we all know when we have formed a letter perfectly; and a stupid artist, right or wrong, is almost equally certain he has found a right tone or a right colour, or made a dexterous stroke with his brush. And, again, painters may work out of doors; and the fresh air, the deliberate seasons, and the "tranquillising influence" of the green earth, counterbalance the fever of thought, and keep them cool, placable, and prosaic.

A ship captain is a good man to marry if it is a marriage of love, for absences are a good influence in love and keep it bright and delicate; but he is just the worst man if the feeling is more pedestrian, as habit is too frequently torn open and the solder has never time to set. Men who fish, botanise, work with the turning-lathe, or gather sea-weeds, will make admirable husbands; and a little amateur painting in water-colour shows the innocent and quiet mind. Those who have a few intimates are to be avoided; while those who swim loose, who have their hat in their hand all along the street, who can number an infinity of acquaintances and are not chargeable with any one friend, promise an easy disposition and no rival to the wife's influence. I will not say they are the best of men, but they are the stuff out of which adroit and capable women manufacture the best of husbands. It is to be noticed that those who have loved once or twice already are so much the better educated to a woman's hand; the bright boy of fiction is an odd and most uncomfortable mixture of shyness and coarseness, and needs a deal of civilising. Lastly (and this is, perhaps, the golden rule), no woman should marry a teetotaller, or a man who does not smoke. It is not for nothing that this "ignoble tabagie," as Michelet calls it, spreads over all the world. Michelet rails against it because it renders you happy apart from thought or work; to provident women this will seem no evil influence in married life. Whatever keeps a man in the front garden, whatever checks wandering fancy and all inordinate ambition, whatever makes for lounging and contentment, makes just so surely for domestic happiness.

These notes, if they amuse the reader at all, will probably amuse him more when he differs than when he agrees with them; at least they will do no harm, for nobody will follow my advice. But the last word is of more concern. Marriage is a step so grave and decisive that it attracts light-headed, variable men by its very awfulness. They have been so tried among the inconstant squalls and currents, so often sailed for islands in the air or lain becalmed with burning heart, that they will risk all for solid ground below their feet. Desperate pilots, they run their sea-sick, weary bark upon the dashing rocks. It seems as if marriage were the royal road through life, and realised, on the instant, what we have all dreamed on summer Sundays when the bells ring, or at night when we cannot sleep for the desire of living. They think it will sober and change them. Like those who join a brotherhood, they fancy it needs but an act to be out of the coil and clamour for ever. But this is a wile of the devil's. To the end, spring winds will sow disquietude, passing faces leave a regret behind them, and the whole world keep calling and calling in their ears. For marriage is like life in this—that it is a field of battle, and not a bed of roses.

## II

HOPE, they say, deserts us at no period of our existence. From first to last, and in the face of smarting disillusions, we continue to expect good fortune, better health, and better conduct; and that so confidently, that we judge it needless to deserve them. I think it improbable that I shall ever write like Shakespeare, conduct an army like Hannibal, or distinguish myself like Marcus Aurelius in the paths of virtue; and yet I have my by-days, hope prompting, when I am very ready to believe that I shall combine all these various excellences in my own person, and go marching down to posterity with divine honours. There is nothing so monstrous but we can believe it of ourselves. About ourselves, about our aspirations and delinquencies, we have dwelt by choice in a delicious vagueness from our boyhood up. No one will have forgotten Tom Sawyer's aspiration: "Ah, if he could only die *temporarily!*" Or, perhaps, better still, the inward resolution of the two pirates, that "so long as they remained in that business, their piracies should not again be sullied with the crime of stealing." Here we recognise the thoughts of our boyhood; and our boyhood ceased—well, when?—not, I think, at twenty; nor, perhaps, altogether at twenty-five; nor yet at thirty; and possibly, to be quite frank, we are still in the thick of that arcadian period. For as the race of man, after centuries of civilisation, still keeps some traits of their barbarian fathers, so man the individual is not altogether quit of youth, when he is already old and honoured, and Lord Chancellor of England. We advance in years somewhat in the manner of an invading army in a barren land; the age that we have reached, as the phrase goes, we but hold with an outpost, and still keep open our communications with the extreme rear and first beginnings of the march. There is our true base; that is not only the beginning, but the perennial spring of our faculties; and grandfather William can retire upon occasion into the green enchanted forest of his boyhood.

The unfading boyishness of hope and its vigorous irrationality are nowhere better displayed than in questions of conduct. There is a character in the *Pilgrim's Progress*, one Mr. *Linger-after-Lust*, with whom I fancy we are all on speaking terms; one famous among the famous for ingenuity of hope up to and beyond the moment of defeat; one who, after eighty years of contrary experience, will believe it possible to continue in the business of piracy and yet avoid the guilt of theft. Every sin is our last; every 1st of January a remarkable turning-point in our career. Any overt act, above all, is felt to be alchemic in its power to change. A drunkard takes the pledge; it will be strange if that does not help him. For how many years did Mr. Pepys continue to make and break his little vows? And yet I have not heard that he was discouraged in the end. By such steps we think to fix a momentary resolution; as a timid fellow hies him to the dentist's while the tooth is stinging.

But, alas, by planting a stake at the top of flood, you can neither prevent nor delay the inevitable ebb. There is no hocus-pocus in morality; and even the "sanctimonious ceremony" of marriage leaves the man unchanged. This is a hard saying, and has an air of paradox. For there is something in marriage so natural and inviting, that the step has an air of great simplicity and ease; it offers to bury for ever many aching pre-occupations; it is to afford us unfailing and familiar company through life; it opens up a smiling prospect of the blest and passive kind of love, rather than the blessing and active; it is approached not only through the delights of courtship, but by a public performance and repeated legal signatures. A man naturally thinks it will go hard with him if he cannot be good and fortunate and happy within such august circumvallations.

And yet there is probably no other act in a man's life so hot-headed and foolhardy as this one of marriage. For years, let us suppose, you have been making the most indifferent business of your career. Your experience has not, we may dare to say, been more encouraging than Paul's or Horace's; like them, you have seen and desired the good that you were not able to accomplish; like them, you have done the evil that you loathed. You have waked at night in a hot or a cold sweat, according to your habit of body, remembering, with dismal surprise, your own unpardonable acts and sayings. You have been sometimes tempted to withdraw entirely from this game of life; as a man who makes nothing but misses withdraws from that less dangerous one of billiards. You have fallen back upon the thought that you yourself most sharply smarted for your misdemeanours, or, in the old, plaintive phrase, that you were nobody's enemy but your own. And then you have been made aware of what was beautiful and amiable, wise and kind, in the other part of your behaviour; and it seemed as if nothing could reconcile the contradiction, as indeed nothing can. If you are a man, you have shut your mouth hard and said nothing; and if you are only a man in the making, you have recognised that yours was quite a special case, and you yourself not guilty of your own pestiferous career.

Granted, and with all my heart. Let us accept these apologies; let us agree that you are nobody's enemy but your own; let us agree that you are a sort of moral cripple, impotent for good; and let us regard you with the unmingled pity due to such a fate. But there is one thing to which, on these terms, we can never agree:— we can never agree to have you marry. What! you have had one life to manage, and have failed so strangely, and now can see nothing wiser than to conjoin with it the management of some one else's? Because you have been unfaithful in a very little, you propose yourself to be a ruler over ten cities. You strip yourself by such a step of all remaining consolations and excuses. You are no longer content to be your own enemy; you must be your wife's also. You have been hitherto in a mere subaltern attitude; dealing cruel blows about you in life, yet only half responsible, since you came there by no choice or movement of your own. Now, it appears, you must take things on your own authority: God made you, but you marry yourself; and for all that your wife suffers, no one is responsible but you. A man must be very certain of his knowledge ere he undertake to guide a ticket-of-leave man through a dangerous pass; you have eternally missed your way in life, with consequences that you still deplore, and yet you masterfully seize your wife's hand, and, blindfold, drag her after you to ruin. And it is your wife, you observe, whom you select. She, whose happiness you most desire, you choose to be your victim.

You would earnestly warn her from a tottering bridge or bad investment. If she were to marry some one else, how you would tremble for her fate! If she were only your sister, and you thought half as much of her, how doubtfully would you entrust her future to a man no better than yourself!

Times are changed with him who marries; there are no more by-path meadows, where you may innocently linger, but the road lies long and straight and dusty to the grave. Idleness which is often becoming and even wise in the bachelor, begins to wear a different aspect when you have a wife to support. Suppose, after you are married, one of those little slips were to befall you. What happened last November might surely happen February next. They may have annoyed you at the time, because they were not what you had meant; but how will they annoy you in the future, and how will they shake the fabric of your wife's confidence and peace! A thousand things unpleasing went on in the *chiaroscuro* of a life that you shrank from too particularly realising; you did not care, in those days, to make a fetish of your conscience; you would recognise your failures with a nod, and so, good day. But the time for these reserves is over. You have wilfully introduced a witness into your life, the scene of these defeats, and can no longer close the mind's eye upon uncomely passages, but must stand up straight and put a name upon your actions. And your witness is not only the judge, but the victim of your sins; not only can she condemn you to the sharpest penalties, but she must herself share feelingly in their endurance. And observe, once more, with what temerity you have chosen precisely *her* to be your spy, whose esteem you value highest, and whom you have already taught to think you better than you are. You may think you had a conscience, and believed in God; but what is a conscience to a wife? Wise men of yore erected statues of their deities, and consciously performed their part in life before those marble eyes. A god watched them at the board, and stood by their bedside in the morning when they woke; and all about their ancient cities, where they bought and sold, or where they piped and wrestled, there would stand some symbol of the things that are outside of man. These were lessons, delivered in the quiet dialect of art, which told their story faithfully, but gently. It is the same lesson, if you will—but how harrowingly taught!—when the woman you respect shall weep from your unkindness or blush with shame at your misconduct. Poor girls in Italy turn their painted Madonnas to the wall: you cannot set aside your wife. To marry is to domesticate the Recording Angel. Once you are married, there is nothing left for you, not even suicide, but to be good.

And goodness in marriage is a more intricate problem than mere single virtue; for in marriage there are two ideals to be realised. A girl, it is true, has always lived in a glass house among reproving relatives, whose word was law; she has been bred up to sacrifice her judgments and take the key submissively from dear papa; and it is wonderful how swiftly she can change her tune into the husband's. Her morality has been, too often, an affair of precept and conformity. But in the case of a bachelor who has enjoyed some measure both of privacy and freedom, his moral judgments have been passed in some accordance with his nature. His sins were always sins in his own sight; he could then only sin when he did some act against his clear conviction; the light that he walked by was obscure, but it was single. Now, when two people of any grit and spirit put their fortunes into one, there succeeds to this comparative certainty a huge welter of competing jurisdictions. It no longer matters so much how life appears to one; one must consult another: one, who may be strong, must not offend the other, who is weak. The only weak brother I am willing to consider is (to make a bull for once), my wife. For her, and for her only, I must waive my righteous judgments, and go crookedly about my life. How, then, in such an atmosphere of compromise, to keep honour bright and abstain from base capitulations? How are you to put aside love's pleadings? How are you, the apostle of laxity, to turn suddenly about into the rabbi of precision; and after these years of ragged practice, pose for a hero to the lackey who has found you out? In this temptation to mutual indulgence lies the particular peril to morality in married life. Daily they drop a little lower from the first ideal, and for a while continue to accept these changelings with a gross complacency. At last Love wakes and looks about him; finds his hero sunk into a stout old brute, intent on brandy pawnee; finds his heroine divested of her angel brightness; and in the flash of that first disenchantment, flees for ever.

Again, the husband, in these unions, is usually a man, and the wife commonly enough a woman; and when this is the case, although it makes the firmer marriage, a thick additional veil of misconception hangs above the doubtful business. Women, I believe, are somewhat rarer than men; but then, if I were a woman myself, I daresay I should hold the reverse; and at least we all enter more or less wholly into one or other of these camps. A man who delights women by his feminine perceptions will often scatter his admirers by a chance explosion of the under side of man; and the most masculine and direct of women will some day, to your dire surprise, draw out like a telescope into successive lengths of personation. Alas! for the man, knowing her to be at heart more candid than himself, who shall flounder, panting, through these mazes in the quest for truth. The proper qualities of each sex are, indeed, eternally surprising to the other. Between the Latin and the Teuton races there are similar divergences, not to be bridged by the most liberal sympathy. And in the good, plain, cut-and-dry explanations of this life, which pass current among us as the wisdom of the elders, this difficulty has been turned with the aid of pious lies. Thus, when a young lady has angelic features, eats nothing to speak of, plays all day long on the piano, and sings ravishingly in church, it requires a rough infidelity, falsely called cynicism, to believe that she may be a little devil after all. Yet so it is: she may be a talebearer, a liar, and a thief; she may have a taste for brandy, and no heart. My compliments to George Eliot for her Rosamond Vincy; the ugly work of satire she has transmuted to the ends of art, by the companion figure of Lydgate; and the satire was much wanted for the education of young men. That doctrine of the excellence of women, however chivalrous, is cowardly as well as false. It is better to face the fact, and know, when you marry, that you take into your life a creature of equal, if of unlike, frailties; whose weak human heart beats no more tunefully than yours.

But it is the object of a liberal education not only to obscure the knowledge of one sex by another, but to magnify the natural differences between the two. Man is a creature who lives not upon bread alone, but principally by catchwords; and the little rift between the sexes is astonishingly widened by simply teaching one set of catchwords to the girls and another to the boys. To the first, there is shown but a very small field of experience, and taught a very trenchant principle for judgment and action; to the other, the world of life is more largely displayed, and their rule of conduct is proportionally widened. They are taught to follow different virtues, to hate different vices, to place their ideal, even for each other, in different achievements. What should be the result of such a course? When a horse has run away, and the two flustered people in the gig have each possessed themselves of a rein, we know the end of that conveyance will be in the ditch. So, when I see a raw youth and a green girl, fluted and fiddled in a dancing measure into that most serious contract, and setting out upon life's journey with ideas so monstrously divergent, I am not surprised that some make shipwreck, but that any come to port. What the boy does almost proudly, as a manly peccadillo, the girl will shudder at as a debasing vice; what is to her the mere common sense of tactics, he will spit out of his mouth as shameful. Through such a sea of contrarieties must this green couple steer their way; and contrive to love each other; and to respect, forsooth; and be ready, when the time arrives, to educate the little men and women who shall succeed to their places and perplexities.

And yet, when all has been said, the man who should hold back from marriage is in the same case with him who runs away from battle. To avoid an occasion for our virtues is a worse degree of failure than to push forward pluckily and make a fall. It is lawful to pray God that we be not led into temptation; but not lawful to skulk from those that come to us. The noblest passage in one of the noblest books of this century, is where the old pope glories in the trial, nay, in the partial fall and but imperfect triumph, of the younger hero.[1] Without some such manly note, it were perhaps better to have no conscience at all. But there is a vast difference between teaching flight, and showing points of peril that a man may march the more warily. And the true conclusion of this paper is to turn our back on apprehensions, and embrace that shining and courageous virtue, Faith. Hope is the boy, a blind, headlong, pleasant fellow, good to chase swallows with the salt; Faith is the grave, experienced, yet smiling man. Hope lives on ignorance; open-eyed Faith is built upon a knowledge of our life, of the tyranny of circumstance and the frailty of human resolution. Hope looks for unqualified success; but Faith counts certainly on failure, and takes honourable defeat to be a form of victory. Hope is a kind old pagan; but Faith grew up in Christian days, and early learnt humility. In the one temper, a man is indignant that he cannot spring up in a clap to heights of elegance and virtue; in the other, out of a sense of his infirmities, he is filled with confidence because a year has come and gone, and he has still preserved some rags of honour. In the first, he expects an angel for a wife; in the last, he knows that she is like himself—erring, thoughtless, and untrue; but like himself also, filled with a struggling radiancy of better things, and adorned with ineffective qualities. You may safely go to school with hope; but ere you marry, should have learned the mingled lesson of the world: that dolls are stuffed with sawdust,

[1] Browning's *Ring and Book.*

and yet are excellent playthings; that hope and love address themselves to a perfection never realised, and yet, firmly held, become the salt and staff of life; that you yourself are compacted of infirmities, perfect, you might say, in imperfection, and yet you have a something in you lovable and worth preserving; and that, while the mass of mankind lies under this scurvy condemnation, you will scarce find one but, by some generous reading, will become to you a lesson, a model, and a noble spouse through life. So thinking, you will constantly support your own unworthiness, and easily forgive the failings of your friend. Nay, you will be wisely glad that you retain the sense of blemishes; for the faults of married people continually spur up each of them, hour by hour, to do better and to meet and love upon a higher ground. And ever, between the failures, there will come glimpses of kind virtues to encourage and console.

# III.—ON FALLING IN LOVE

"Lord, what fools these mortals be!"

There is only one event in life which really astonishes a man and startles him out of his prepared opinions. Everything else befalls him very much as he expected. Event succeeds to event, with an agreeable variety indeed, but with little that is either startling or intense; they form together no more than a sort of background, or running accompaniment to the man's own reflections; and he falls naturally into a cool, curious, and smiling habit of mind, and builds himself up in a conception of life which expects to-morrow to be after the pattern of to-day and yesterday. He may be accustomed to the vagaries of his friends and acquaintances under the influence of love. He may sometimes look forward to it for himself with an incomprehensible expectation. But it is a subject in which neither intuition nor the behaviour of others will help the philosopher to the truth. There is probably nothing rightly thought or rightly written on this matter of love that is not a piece of the person's experience. I remember an anecdote of a well-known French theorist, who was debating a point eagerly in his *cénacle*. It was objected against him that he had never experienced love. Whereupon he arose, left the society, and made it a point not to return to it until he considered that he had supplied the defect. "Now," he remarked, on entering, "now I am in a position to continue the discussion." Perhaps he had not penetrated very deeply into the subject after all; but the story indicates right thinking, and may serve as an apologue to readers of this essay.

When at last the scales fall from his eyes, it is not without something of the nature of dismay that the man finds himself in such changed conditions. He has to deal with commanding emotions instead of the easy dislikes and preferences in which he has hitherto passed his days; and he recognises capabilities for pain and pleasure of which he had not yet suspected the existence. Falling in love is the one illogical adventure, the one thing of which we are tempted to think as supernatural, in our trite and reasonable world. The effect is out of all proportion with the cause. Two persons, neither of them, it may be, very amiable or very beautiful, meet, speak a little, and look a little into each other's eyes. That has been done a dozen or so of times in the experience of either with no great result. But on this occasion all is different. They fall at once into that state in which another person becomes to us the very gist and centre-point of God's creation, and demolishes our laborious theories with a smile; in which our ideas are so bound up with the one master-thought that even the trivial cares of our own person become so many acts of devotion, and the love of life itself is translated into a wish to remain in the same world with so precious and desirable a fellow-creature. And all the while their acquaintances look on in stupor, and ask each other, with almost passionate emphasis, what so-and-so can see in that woman, or such-an-one in that man? I am sure, gentlemen, I cannot tell you. For my part, I cannot think what the women mean. It might be very well, if the Apollo Belvedere should suddenly glow all over into life, and step forward from the pedestal with that godlike air of his. But of the misbegotten changelings who call themselves men, and prate intolerably over dinner-table, I never saw one who seemed worthy to inspire love—no, nor read of any, except Leonardo da Vinci, and perhaps Goethe in his youth. About women I entertain a somewhat different opinion; but there, I have the misfortune to be a man.

There are many matters in which you may waylay Destiny, and bid him stand and deliver. Hard work, high thinking, adventurous excitement, and a great deal more that forms a part of this or the other person's spiritual bill of fare, are within the reach of almost any one who can dare a little and be patient. But it is by no means in the way of every one to fall in love. You know the difficulty Shakespeare was put into when Queen Elizabeth asked him to show Falstaff in love. I do not believe that Henry Fielding was ever in love. Scott, if it were not for a passage or two in *Rob Roy*, would give me very much the same effect. These are great names and (what is more to the purpose) strong, healthy, high-strung, and generous natures, of whom the reverse might have been expected. As for the innumerable army of anæmic and tailorish persons who occupy the face of this planet with so much propriety, it is palpably absurd to imagine them in any such situation as a love-affair. A wet rag goes safely by the fire; and if a man is blind, he cannot expect to be much impressed by romantic scenery. Apart from all this many lovable people miss each other in the world, or meet under some unfavourable star. There is the nice and critical moment of declaration to be got over. From timidity or lack of opportunity a good half of possible love cases never get so far, and at least another quarter do there cease and determine. A very adroit person, to be sure, manages to prepare the way and out with his declaration in the nick of time. And then there is a fine solid sort of man, who goes on from snub to snub; and if he has to declare forty times, will continue imperturbably declaring, amid the astonished consideration of men and angels, until he has a favourable answer. I daresay, if one were a woman, one would like to marry a man who was capable of doing this, but not quite one who had done so. It is just a little bit abject, and somehow just a little bit gross; and marriages in which one of the parties has been thus battered into consent scarcely form agreeable subjects for meditation. Love should run out to meet love with open arms. Indeed, the ideal story is that of two people who go into love step for step, with a fluttered consciousness, like a pair of children venturing together into a dark room. From the first moment when they see each other, with a pang of curiosity, through stage after stage of growing pleasure and embarrassment, they can read the expression of their own trouble in each other's eyes. There is here no declaration properly so called; the feeling is so plainly shared, that as soon as the man knows what it is in his own heart, he is sure of what it is in the woman's.

This simple accident of falling in love is as beneficial as it is astonishing. It arrests the petrifying influence of years, disproves cold-blooded and cynical conclusions, and awakens dormant sensibilities. Hitherto the man had found it a good policy to disbelieve the existence of any enjoyment which was out of his reach; and thus he turned his back upon the strong sunny parts of nature, and accustomed himself to look exclusively on what was common and dull. He accepted a prose ideal, let himself go blind of many sympathies by disuse; and if he were young and witty, or beautiful, wilfully forwent these advantages. He joined himself to the following of what, in the old mythology of love, was prettily called *nonchaloir;* and in an odd mixture of feelings, a fling of self-respect, a preference for selfish liberty, and a great dash of that fear with which honest people regard serious interests, kept himself back from the straightforward course of life among certain selected activities. And now, all of a sudden, he is unhorsed, like St. Paul, from his infidel affectation. His heart, which has been ticking accurate seconds for the last year, gives a bound and begins to beat high and irregularly in his breast. It seems as if he had never heard or felt or seen until that moment; and by the report of his memory, he must have lived his past life between sleep and waking, or with the pre-occupied attention of a brown study. He is practically incommoded by the generosity of his feelings, smiles much when he is alone, and develops a habit of looking rather blankly upon the moon and stars. But it is not at all within the province of a prose essayist to give a picture of this hyperbolical frame of mind; and the thing has been done already, and that to admiration. In *Adelaide*, in Tennyson's *Maud*, and in some of Heine's songs, you get the absolute expression of this midsummer spirit. Romeo and Juliet were very much in love; although they tell me some German critics are of a different opinion, probably the same who would have us think Mercutio a dull fellow. Poor Antony was in love, and no mistake. That lay figure Marius, in *Les Misérables*, is also a genuine case in his own way, and worth observation. A good many of George Sand's people are thoroughly in love; and so are a good many of George Meredith's. Altogether, there is plenty to read on the subject. If the root of the matter be in him, and if he has the requisite chords to set in vibration, a young man may occasionally enter, with the key of art, into that land of Beulah which is upon the borders of Heaven and within sight of the City of Love. There let him sit awhile to hatch delightful hopes and perilous illusions.

One thing that accompanies the passion in its first blush is certainly difficult to explain. It comes (I do not quite see how, that from having a very supreme sense of pleasure in all parts of life—in lying down to sleep, in waking, in motion, in breathing, in continuing to be—the lover begins to regard his happiness as beneficial for the rest of the world and highly meritorious in himself. Our race has never been able contentedly to suppose that the noise of its wars, conducted by a few young gentlemen in a corner of an inconsiderable star, does not re-echo among the courts of Heaven with quite a formidable effect. In much the same taste, when people find a great to-do in their own breasts, they imagine it must have some influence in their neighbourhood. The presence of the two lovers is so enchanting to each other that it seems as if it must be the best thing possible for everybody else. They are half inclined to fancy it is because of them and their love that the sky is blue and the sun shines. And certainly the weather is usually fine while people are courting. . . . In point of fact, although the happy man feels very kindly towards others of his own sex, there is apt to be something too much of the magnifico in his demeanour. If people grow presuming and self-important over such matters as a dukedom or the

Holy See, they will scarcely support the dizziest elevation in life without some suspicion of a strut; and the dizziest elevation is to love and be loved in return. Consequently, accepted lovers are a trifle condescending in their address to other men. An overweening sense of the passion and importance of life hardly conduces to simplicity of manner. To women, they feel very nobly, very purely, and very generously, as if they were so many Joan-of-Arcs; but this does not come out in their behaviour; and they treat them to Grandisonian airs marked with a suspicion of fatuity. I am not quite certain that women do not like this sort of thing; but really, after having bemused myself over *Daniel Deronda*, I have given up trying to understand what they like.

If it did nothing else, this sublime and ridiculous superstition, that the pleasure of the pair is somehow blessed to others, and everybody is made happier in their happiness, would serve at least to keep love generous and great-hearted. Nor is it quite a baseless superstition after all. Other lovers are hugely interested. They strike the nicest balance between pity and approval, when they see people aping the greatness of their own sentiments. It is an understood thing in the play, that while the young gentlefolk are courting on the terrace, a rough flirtation is being carried on, and a light, trivial sort of love is growing up, between the footman and the singing chambermaid. As people are generally cast for the leading parts in their own imaginations, the reader can apply the parallel to real life without much chance of going wrong. In short, they are quite sure this other love-affair is not so deep-seated as their own, but they like dearly to see it going forward. And love, considered as a spectacle, must have attractions for many who are not of the confraternity. The sentimental old maid is a commonplace of the novelists; and he must be rather a poor sort of human being, to be sure, who can look on at this pretty madness without indulgence and sympathy. For nature commends itself to people with a most insinuating art; the busiest is now and again arrested by a great sunset; and you may be as pacific or as cold-blooded as you will, but you cannot help some emotion when you read of well-disputed battles, or meet a pair of lovers in the lane.

Certainly, whatever it may be with regard to the world at large, this idea of beneficent pleasure is true as between the sweethearts. To do good and communicate is the lover's grand intention. It is the happiness of the other that makes his own most intense gratification. It is not possible to disentangle the different emotions, the pride, humility, pity and passion, which are excited by a look of happy love or an unexpected caress. To make one's self beautiful, to dress the hair, to excel in talk, to do anything and all things that puff out the character and attributes and make them imposing in the eyes of others, is not only to magnify one's self, but to offer the most delicate homage at the same time. And it is in this latter intention that they are done by lovers; for the essence of love is kindness; and indeed it may be best defined as passionate kindness: kindness, so to speak, run mad and become importunate and violent. Vanity in a merely personal sense exists no longer. The lover takes a perilous pleasure in privately displaying his weak points and having them, one after another, accepted and condoned. He wishes to be assured that he is not loved for this or that good quality, but for himself, or something as like himself as he can contrive to set forward.

For, although it may have been a very difficult thing to paint the marriage of Cana, or write the fourth act of Antony and Cleopatra, there is a more difficult piece of art before every one in this world who cares to set about explaining his own character to others. Words and acts are easily wrenched from their true significance; and they are all the language we have to come and go upon. A pitiful job we make of it, as a rule. For better or worse, people mistake our meaning and take our emotions at a wrong valuation. And generally we rest pretty content with our failures; we are content to be misapprehended by crackling flirts; but when once a man is moonstruck with this affection of love, he makes it a point of honour to clear such dubieties away. He cannot have the Best of her Sex misled upon a point of this importance; and his pride revolts at being loved in a mistake.

He discovers a great reluctance to return on former periods of his life. To all that has not been shared with her, rights and duties, bygone fortunes and dispositions, he can look back only by a difficult and repugnant effort of the will. That he should have wasted some years in ignorance of what alone was really important, that he may have entertained the thought of other women with any show of complacency, is a burthen almost too heavy for his self-respect. But it is the thought of another past that rankles in his spirit like a poisoned wound. That he himself made a fashion of being alive in the bald, beggarly days before a certain meeting, is deplorable enough in all good conscience. But that She should have permitted herself the same liberty seems inconsistent with a Divine providence.

A great many people run down jealousy, on the score that it is an artificial feeling, as well as practically inconvenient. This is scarcely fair; for the feeling on which it merely attends, like an ill-humoured courtier, is itself artificial in exactly the same sense and to the same degree. I suppose what is meant by that objection is that jealousy has not always been a character of man; formed no part of that very modest kit of sentiments with which he is supposed to have begun the world: but waited to make its appearance in better days and among richer natures. And this is equally true of love, and friendship, and love of country, and delight in what they call the beauties of nature, and most other things worth having. Love, in particular, will not endure any historical scrutiny: to all who have fallen across it, it is one of the most incontestable facts in the world; but if you begin to ask what it was in other periods and countries, in Greece for instance, the strangest doubts begin to spring up, and everything seems so vague and changing that a dream is logical in comparison. Jealousy, at any rate, is one of the consequences of love; you may like it or not, at pleasure; but there it is.

It is not exactly jealousy, however, that we feel when we reflect on the past of those we love. A bundle of letters found after years of happy union creates no sense of insecurity in the present; and yet it will pain a man sharply. The two people entertain no vulgar doubt of each other: but this pre-existence of both occurs to the mind as something indelicate. To be altogether right, they should have had twin birth together, at the same moment with the feeling that unites them. Then indeed it would be simple and perfect and without reserve or afterthought. Then they would understand each other with a fulness impossible otherwise. There would be no barrier between them of associations that cannot be imparted. They would be led into none of those comparisons that send the blood back to the heart. And they would know that there had been no time lost, and they had been together as much as was possible. For besides terror for the separation that must follow some time or other in the future, men feel anger, and something like remorse, when they think of that other separation which endured until they met. Some one has written that love makes people believe in immortality, because there seems not to be room enough in life for so great a tenderness, and it is inconceivable that the most masterful of our emotions should have no more than the spare moments of a few years. Indeed, it seems strange ; but if we call to mind analogies, we can hardly regard it as impossible.

"The blind bow-boy," who smiles upon us from the end of terraces in old Dutch gardens, laughingly hails his bird-bolts among a fleeting generation. But for as fast as ever he shoots, the game dissolves and disappears into eternity from under his falling arrows ; this one is gone ere he is struck ; the other has but time to make one gesture and give one passionate cry ; and they are all the things of a moment. When the generation is gone, when the play is over, when the thirty years' panorama has been withdrawn in tatters from the stage of the world, we may ask what has become of these great, weighty, and undying loves, and the sweethearts who despised mortal conditions in a fine credulity ; and they can only show us a few songs in a bygone taste, a few actions worth remembering, and a few children who have retained some happy stamp from the disposition of their parents.

## IV.—TRUTH OF INTERCOURSE

AMONG sayings that have a currency in spite of being wholly false upon the face of them for the sake of a half-truth upon another subject which is accidentally combined with the error, one of the grossest and broadest conveys the monstrous proposition that it is easy to tell the truth and hard to tell a lie. I wish heartily it were. But the truth is one; it has first to be discovered, then justly and exactly uttered. Even with instruments specially contrived for such a purpose—with a foot-rule, a level, or a theodolite—it is not easy to be exact; it is easier, alas! to be inexact. From those who mark the divisions on a scale to those who measure the boundaries of empires or the distance of the heavenly stars, it is by careful method and minute, unwearying attention that men rise even to material exactness or to sure knowledge even of external and constant things. But it is easier to draw the outline of a mountain than the changing appearance of a face; and truth in human relations is of this more intangible and dubious order: hard to seize, harder to communicate. Veracity to facts in a loose, colloquial sense—not to say that I have been in Malabar when as a matter of fact I was never out of England, not to say that I have read Cervantes in the original when as a matter of fact I know not one syllable of Spanish—this, indeed, is easy and to the same degree unimportant in itself. Lies of this sort, according to circumstances, may or may not be important; in a certain sense even they may or may not be false. The habitual liar may be a very honest fellow, and live truly with his wife and friends; while another man who never told a formal falsehood in his life may yet be himself one lie—heart and face, from top to bottom. This is the kind of lie which poisons intimacy. And, *vice versâ*, veracity to sentiment, truth in a relation, truth to your own heart and your friends, never to feign or falsify emotion—that is the truth which makes love possible and mankind happy.

*L'art de bien dire* is but a drawing-room accomplishment unless it be pressed into the service of the truth. The difficulty of literature is not to write, but to write what you mean; not to affect your reader, but to affect him precisely as you wish. This is commonly understood in the case of books or set orations; even in making your will, or writing an explicit letter, some difficulty is admitted by the world. But one thing you can never make Philistine natures understand; one thing, which yet lies on the surface, remains as unseizable to their wits as a high flight of metaphysics—namely, that the business of life is mainly carried on by means of this difficult art of literature, and according to a man's proficiency in that art shall be the freedom and the fulness of his intercourse with other men. Anybody, it is supposed, can say what he means; and, in spite of their notorious experience to the contrary, people so continue to suppose. Now, I simply open the last book I have been reading—Mr. Leland's captivating *English Gipsies*. "It is said," I find on p. 7, "that those who can converse with Irish peasants in their own native tongue form far higher opinions of their appreciation of the beautiful, and of *the elements of humour and pathos in their hearts*, than do those who know their thoughts only through the medium of English. I know from my own observations that this is quite the case with the Indians of North America, and it is unquestionably so with the gipsy." In short, where a man has not a full possession of the language, the most important, because the most amiable, qualities of his nature have to lie buried and fallow; for the pleasure of comradeship, and the intellectual part of love, rest upon these very "elements of humour and pathos." Here is a man opulent in both, and for lack of a medium he can put none of it out to interest in the market of affection! But what is thus made plain to our apprehensions in the case of a foreign language is partially true even with the tongue we learned in childhood. Indeed, we all speak different dialects; one shall be copious and exact, another loose and meagre; but the speech of the ideal talker shall correspond and fit upon the truth of fact—not clumsily, obscuring lineaments, like a mantle, but cleanly adhering, like an athlete's skin. And what is the result? That the one can open himself more clearly to his friends, and can enjoy more of what makes life truly valuable—intimacy with those he loves. An orator makes a false step; he employs some trivial, some absurd, some vulgar phrase; in the turn of a sentence he insults, by a side wind, those whom he is labouring to charm; in speaking to one sentiment he unconsciously ruffles another in parenthesis; and you are not surprised, for you know his task to be delicate and filled with perils. "O frivolous mind of man, light ignorance!" As if yourself, when you seek to explain some misunderstanding or excuse some apparent fault, speaking swiftly and addressing a mind still recently incensed, were not harnessing for a more perilous adventure; as if yourself required less tact and eloquence; as if an angry friend or a suspicious lover were not more easy to offend than a meeting of indifferent politicians! Nay, and the orator treads in a beaten round; the matters he discusses have been discussed a thousand times before; language is ready-shaped to his purpose; he speaks out of a cut and dry vocabulary. But you—may it not be that your defence reposes on some subtlety of feeling, not so much as touched upon in Shakespeare, to express which, like a pioneer, you must venture forth into zones of thought still unsurveyed, and become yourself a literary innovator? For even in love there are unlovely humours; ambiguous acts, unpardonable words, may yet have sprung from a kind sentiment. If the injured one could read your heart, you may be sure that he would understand and pardon; but, alas! the heart cannot be shown—it has to be demonstrated in words. Do you think it is a hard thing to write poetry? Why, that is to write poetry, and of a high, if not the highest, order.

I should even more admire "the lifelong and heroic literary labours" of my fellow-men, patiently clearing up in words their loves and their contentions, and speaking their autobiography daily to their wives, were it not for a circumstance which lessens their difficulty and my admiration by equal parts. For life, though largely, is not entirely carried on by literature. We are subject to physical passions and contortions; the voice breaks and changes, and speaks by unconscious and winning inflections; we have legible countenances, like an open book; things that cannot be said look eloquently through the eyes; and the soul, not locked into the body as a dungeon, dwells ever on the threshold with appealing signals. Groans and tears, looks and gestures, a flush or a paleness, are often the most clear reporters of the heart, and speak more directly to the hearts of others. The message flies by these interpreters in the least space of time, and the misunderstanding is averted in the moment of its birth. To explain in words takes time and a just and patient hearing; and in the critical epochs of a close relation, patience and justice are not qualities on which we can rely. But the look or the gesture explains things in a breath; they tell their message without ambiguity; unlike speech, they cannot stumble, by the way, on a reproach or an allusion that should steel your friend against the truth; and then they have a higher authority, for they are the direct expression of the heart, not yet transmitted through the unfaithful and sophisticating brain. Not long ago I wrote a letter to a friend which came near involving us in quarrel; but we met, and in personal talk I repeated the worst of what I had written, and added worse to that; and with the commentary of the body it seemed not unfriendly either to hear or say. Indeed, letters are in vain for the purposes of intimacy; an absence is a dead break in the relation; yet two who know each other fully and are bent on perpetuity in love, may so preserve the attitude of their affections that they may meet on the same terms as they had parted.

Pitiful is the case of the blind, who cannot read the face; pitiful that of the deaf, who cannot follow the changes of the voice. And there are others also to be pitied; for there are some of an inert, uneloquent nature, who have been denied all the symbols of communication, who have neither a lively play of facial expression, nor speaking gestures, nor a responsive voice, nor yet the gift of frank, explanatory speech: people truly made of clay, people tied for life into a bag which no one can undo. They are poorer than the gipsy, for their heart can speak no language under heaven. Such people we must learn slowly by the tenor of their acts, or through yea and nay communications; or we take them on trust on the strength of a general air, and now and again, when we see the spirit breaking through in a flash, correct or change our estimate. But these will be uphill intimacies, without charm or freedom, to the end; and freedom is the chief ingredient in confidence. Some minds, romantically dull, despise physical endowments. That is a doctrine for a misanthrope; to those who like their fellow-creatures it must always be meaningless; and, for my part, I can see few things more desirable, after the possession of such radical qualities as honour and humour and pathos, than to have a lively and not a stolid countenance; to have looks to correspond with every feeling; to be elegant and delightful in person, so that we shall please even in the intervals of active pleasing, and may never discredit speech with uncouth manners or become unconsciously our own burlesques. But of all unfortunates there is one creature (for I will not call him man) conspicuous in misfortune. This is he who has forfeited his birthright of expression, who has cultivated artful intonations, who has taught his face tricks, like a pet monkey, and on every side perverted or cut off his means of communication with his fellow-men. The body is a house of many windows: there we all sit, showing ourselves and crying on the passers-by to come and love us. But this fellow has filled his windows with opaque glass, elegantly coloured. His house may be admired for its design, the crowd may pause before the stained windows, but meanwhile the poor proprietor must lie languishing within, uncomforted, unchangeably alone.

Truth of intercourse is something more difficult than to refrain from open lies. It is possible to avoid falsehood and yet not tell the truth. It is not enough to answer formal questions. To reach the truth by yea and nay communications implies a questioner with a share of inspiration, such as is often found in mutual love. *Yea* and *nay* mean nothing; the meaning must have been related in the question. Many words are often necessary to convey a very simple statement; for in this sort of exercise we never hit the gold; the most that we can hope is by many arrows, more or less far off on different sides, to indicate, in the course of time, for what target we are aiming, and after an hour's talk, back and forward, to convey the purport of a single principle or a single thought. And yet while the curt, pithy speaker misses the point entirely, a wordy, prolegomenous babbler will often add three new offences in the process of excusing one. It is really a most delicate affair. The world was made before the English language, and seemingly upon a different design. Suppose we held our converse not in words, but in music; those who have a bad ear would find themselves cut off from all near commerce, and no better than foreigners in this big world. But we do not consider how many have "a bad ear" for words, nor how often the most eloquent find nothing to reply. I hate questioners and questions; there are so few that can be spoken to without a lie. "*Do you forgive me?*" Madam and sweetheart, so far as I have gone in life I have never yet been able to discover what forgiveness means. "*Is it still the same between us?*" Why, how can it be? It is eternally different; and yet you are still the friend of my heart. "*Do you understand me?"* God knows; I should think it highly improbable.

The cruellest lies are often told in silence. A man may have sat in a room for hours and not opened his teeth, and yet come out of that room a disloyal friend or a vile calumniator. And how many loves have perished because, from pride, or spite, or diffidence, or that unmanly shame which withholds a man from daring to betray emotion, a lover, at the critical point of the relation, has but hung his head and held his tongue? And, again, a lie may be told by a truth, or a truth conveyed through a lie. Truth to facts is not always truth to sentiment; and part of the truth, as often happens in answer to a question, may be the foulest calumny. A fact may be an exception; but the feeling is the law, and it is that which you must neither garble nor belie. The whole tenor of a conversation is a part of the meaning of each separate statement; the beginning and the end define and travesty the intermediate conversation. You never speak to God; you address a fellow-man, full of his own tempers; and to tell truth, rightly understood, is not to state the true facts, but to convey a true impression; truth in spirit, not truth to letter, is the true veracity. To reconcile averted friends a Jesuitical discretion is often needful, not so much to gain a kind hearing as to communicate sober truth. Women have an ill name in this connection; yet they live in as true relations; the lie of a good woman is the true index of her heart.

"It takes," says Thoreau, in the noblest and most useful passage I remember to have read in any modern author,[1]

[1] *A Week on the Concord and Merrimack Rivers*, Wednesday, p. 283.

"two to speak truth—one to speak and another to hear." He must be very little experienced, or have no great zeal for truth, who does not recognise the fact. A grain of anger or a grain of suspicion produces strange acoustical effects, and makes the ear greedy to remark offence. Hence we find those who have once quarrelled carry themselves distantly, and are ever ready to break the truce. To speak truth there must be moral equality or else no respect; and hence between parent and child intercourse is apt to degenerate into a verbal fencing bout, and misapprehensions to become ingrained. And there is another side to this, for the parent begins with an imperfect notion of the child's character, formed in early years or during the equinoctial gales of youth; to this he adheres, noting only the facts which suit with his preconception; and wherever a person fancies himself unjustly judged, he at once and finally gives up the effort to speak truth. With our chosen friends, on the other hand, and still more between lovers (for mutual understanding is love's essence), the truth is easily indicated by the one and aptly comprehended by the other. A hint taken, a look understood, conveys the gist of long and delicate explanations; and where the life is known even *yea* and *nay* become luminous. In the closest of all relations—that of a love well founded and equally shared—speech is half discarded, like a roundabout, infantile process or a ceremony of formal etiquette; and the two communicate directly by their presences, and with few looks and fewer words contrive to share their good and evil and uphold each other's hearts in joy. For love rests upon a physical basis; it is a familiarity of nature's making and apart from voluntary choice. Understanding has in some sort outrun knowledge, for the affection perhaps began with the acquaintance; and as it was not made like other relations, so it is not, like them, to be perturbed or clouded. Each knows more than can be uttered; each lives by faith, and believes by a natural compulsion; and between man and wife the language of the body is largely developed and grown strangely eloquent. The thought that prompted and was conveyed in a caress would only lose to be set down in words—ay, although Shakespeare himself should be the scribe.

Yet it is in these dear intimacies, beyond all others, that we must strive and do battle for the truth. Let but a doubt arise, and alas! all the previous intimacy and confidence is but another charge against the person doubted. "*What a monstrous dishonesty is this if I have been deceived so long and so completely!*" Let but that thought gain entrance, and you plead before a deaf tribunal. Appeal to the past; why, that is your crime! Make all clear, convince the reason; alas! speciousness is but a proof against you. "*If you can abuse me now, the more likely that you have abused me from the first.*"

For a strong affection such moments are worth supporting, and they will end well; for your advocate is in your lover's heart and speaks her own language; it is not you but she herself who can defend and clear you of the charge. But in slighter intimacies, and for a less stringent union? Indeed, is it worth while? We are all *incompris*, only more or less concerned for the mischance; all trying wrongly to do right; all fawning at each other's feet like dumb, neglected lapdogs. Sometimes we catch an eye—this is our opportunity in the ages—and we wag our tail with a poor smile. "*Is that all?*" All? If you only knew! But how can they know? They do not love us; the more fools we to squander life on the indifferent.

But the morality of the thing, you will be glad to hear, is excellent; for it is only by trying to understand others that we can get our own hearts understood; and in matters of human feeling the clement judge is the most successful pleader.

# CRABBED AGE AND YOUTH

# CRABBED AGE AND YOUTH

"You know my mother now and then argues very notably; always very warmly at least. I happen often to differ from her; and we both think so well of our own arguments, that we very seldom are so happy as to convince one another. A pretty common case, I believe, in all *vehement* debatings. She says, I am *too witty;* Anglicè, *too pert;* I, that she is *too wise;* that is to say, being likewise put into English, *not so young as she has been.*"—Miss Howe to Miss Harlowe, *Clarissa*, vol. ii. Letter xiii.

THERE is a strong feeling in favour of cowardly and prudential proverbs. The sentiments of a man while he is full of ardour and hope are to be received, it is supposed, with some qualification. But when the same person has ignominiously failed and begins to eat up his words, he should be listened to like an oracle. Most of our pocket wisdom is conceived for the use of mediocre people, to discourage them from ambitious attempts, and generally console them in their mediocrity. And since mediocre people constitute the bulk of humanity, this is no doubt very properly so. But it does not follow that the one sort of proposition is any less true than the other, or that Icarus is not to be more praised, and perhaps more envied, than Mr. Samuel Budgett the Successful Merchant. The one is dead, to be sure, while the other is still in his counting-house counting out his money; and doubtless this is a consideration. But we have, on the other hand, some bold and magnanimous sayings common to high races and natures, which set forth the advantage of the losing side, and proclaim it better to be a dead lion than a living dog. It is difficult to fancy how the mediocrities reconcile such sayings with their proverbs. According to the latter, every lad who goes to sea is an egregious ass; never to forget your umbrella through a long life would seem a higher and wiser flight of achievement than to go smiling to the stake; and so long as you are a bit of a coward and inflexible in money matters, you fulfil the whole duty of man.

It is a still more difficult consideration for our average men, that while all their teachers, from Solomon down to Benjamin Franklin and the ungodly Binney, have inculcated the same ideal of manners, caution, and respectability, those characters in history who have most notoriously flown in the face of such precepts are spoken of in hyperbolical terms of praise, and honoured with public monuments in the streets of our commercial centres. This is very bewildering to the moral sense. You have Joan of Arc, who left a humble but honest and reputable livelihood under the eyes of her parents, to go a-colonelling, in the company of rowdy soldiers, against the enemies of France; surely a melancholy example for one's daughters! And then you have Columbus, who may have pioneered America, but, when all is said, was a most imprudent navigator. His Life is not the kind of thing one would like to put into the hands of young people; rather, one would do one's utmost to keep it from their knowledge, as a red flag of adventure and disintegrating influence in life. The time would fail me if I were to recite all the big names in history whose exploits are perfectly irrational and even shocking to the business mind. The incongruity is speaking; and I imagine it must engender among the mediocrities a very peculiar attitude towards the nobler and showier sides of national life. They will read of the Charge of Balaclava in much the same spirit as they assist at a performance of the *Lyons Mail*. Persons of substance take in the *Times* and sit composedly in pit or boxes according to the degree of their prosperity in business. As for the generals who go galloping up and down among bomb-shells in absurd cocked hats—as for the actors who raddle their faces and demean themselves for hire upon the stage—they must belong, thank God! to a different order of beings, whom we watch as we watch the clouds careering in the windy, bottomless inane, or read about like characters in ancient and rather fabulous annals. Our offspring would no more think of copying their behaviour, let us hope, than of doffing their clothes and painting themselves blue in consequence of certain admissions in the first chapter of their school history of England.

Discredited as they are in practice, the cowardly proverbs hold their own in theory; and it is another instance of the same spirit, that the opinions of old men about life have been accepted as final. All sorts of allowances are made for the illusions of youth; and none, or almost none, for the disenchantments of age. It is held to be a good taunt, and somehow or other to clinch the question logically, when an old gentleman waggles his head and says: "Ah, so I thought when I was your age." It is not thought an answer at all, if the young man retorts: "My venerable sir, so I shall most probably think when I am yours." And yet the one is as good as the other: pass for pass, tit for tat, a Roland for an Oliver.

"Opinion in good men," says Milton, "is but knowledge in the making." All opinions, properly so called, are stages on the road to truth. It does not follow that a man will travel any further; but if he has really considered the world and drawn a conclusion, he has travelled as far. This does not apply to formulæ got by rote, which are stages on the road to nowhere but second childhood and the grave. To have a catchword in your mouth is not the same thing as to hold an opinion; still less is it the same thing as to have made one for yourself. There are too many of these catchwords in the world for people to rap out upon you like an oath and by way of an argument. They have a currency as intellectual counters; and many respectable persons pay their way with nothing else. They seem to stand for vague bodies of theory in the background. The imputed virtue of folios full of knockdown arguments is supposed to reside in them, just as some of the majesty of the British Empire dwells in the constable's truncheon. They are used in pure superstition, as old clodhoppers spoil Latin by way of an exorcism. And yet they are vastly serviceable for checking unprofitable discussion and stopping the mouths of babes and sucklings. And when a young man comes to a certain stage of intellectual growth, the examination of these counters forms a gymnastic at once amusing and fortifying to the mind.

Because I have reached Paris, I am not ashamed of having passed through Newhaven and Dieppe. They were very good places to pass through, and I am none the less at my destination. All my old opinions were only stages on the way to the one I now hold, as itself is only a stage on the way to something else. I am no more abashed at having been a red-hot Socialist with a panacea of my own than at having been a sucking infant. Doubtless the world is quite right in a million ways; but you have to be kicked about a little to convince you of the fact. And in the meanwhile you must do something, be something, believe something. It is not possible to keep the mind in a state of accurate balance and blank; and even if you could do so, instead of coming ultimately to the right conclusion, you would be very apt to remain in a state of balance and blank to perpetuity. Even in quite intermediate stages, a dash of enthusiasm is not a thing to be ashamed of in the retrospect; if St. Paul had not been a very zealous Pharisee, he would have been a colder Christian. For my part, I look back to the time when I was a Socialist with something like regret. I have convinced myself (for the moment) that we had better leave these great changes to what we call great blind forces: their blindness being so much more perspicacious than the little, peering, partial eyesight of men. I seem to see that my own scheme would not answer; and all the other schemes I ever heard propounded would depress some elements of goodness just as much as they encouraged others. Now I know that in thus turning Conservative with years, I am going through the normal cycle of change and travelling in the common orbit of men's opinions. I submit to this, as I would submit to gout or gray hair, as a concomitant of growing age or else of failing animal heat; but I do not acknowledge that it is necessarily a change for the better—I daresay it is deplorably for the worse. I have no choice in the business, and can no more resist this tendency of my mind than I could prevent my body from beginning to totter and decay. If I am spared (as the phrase runs) I shall doubtless outlive some troublesome desires; but I am in no hurry about that; nor, when the time comes, shall I plume myself on the immunity. Just in the same way, I do not greatly pride myself on having outlived my belief in the fairy tales of Socialism. Old people have faults of their own; they tend to become cowardly, niggardly, and suspicious. Whether from the growth of experience or the decline of animal heat, I see that age leads to these and certain other faults; and it follows, of course, that while in one sense I hope I am journeying towards the truth, in another I am indubitably posting towards these forms and sources of error.

As we go catching and catching at this or that corner of knowledge, now getting a foresight of generous possibilities, now chilled with a glimpse of prudence, we may compare the headlong course of our years to a swift torrent in which a man is carried away; now he is dashed against a boulder, now he grapples for a moment to a trailing spray; at the end, he is hurled out and overwhelmed in a dark and bottomless ocean. We have no more than glimpses and touches; we are torn away from our theories; we are spun round and round and shown this or the other view of life, until only fools or knaves can hold to their opinions. We take a sight at a condition in life, and say we have studied it; our most elaborate view is no more than an impression. If we had breathing space, we should take the occasion to modify and adjust; but at this breakneck hurry, we are no sooner boys than we are adult, no sooner in love than married or jilted, no sooner one age than we begin to be another, and no sooner in the fulness of our manhood than we begin to decline towards the grave. It is in vain to seek for consistency or expect clear and stable views in a medium so perturbed and fleeting. This is no cabinet science, in which things are tested to a scruple; we theorise with a pistol to our head; we are confronted with a new set of conditions on which we have not only to pass a judgment, but to take action, before the hour is at an end. And we cannot even regard ourselves as a constant; in this flux of things, our identity itself seems in a perpetual variation; and not infrequently we find our own disguise the strangest in the masquerade. In the course of time, we grow to love things we hated and hate things we loved. Milton is not so dull as he once was, nor perhaps Ainsworth so amusing. It is decidedly harder to climb trees, and not nearly so hard to sit still. There is no use pretending; even the thrice royal game of hide and seek has somehow lost in zest. All our attributes are modified or changed; and it will be a poor account of us if our views do not modify and change in a proportion. To hold the same views at forty as we held at twenty is to have been stupefied for a score of years, and take rank, not as a prophet, but as an unteachable brat, well birched and none the wiser. It is as if a ship captain should sail to India from the Port of London; and having brought a chart of the Thames on deck at his first setting out, should obstinately use no other for the whole voyage.

And mark you, it would be no less foolish to begin at Gravesend with a chart of the Red Sea. *Si Jeunesse savait, si Vieillesse pouvait*, is a very pretty sentiment, but not necessarily right. In five cases out of ten, it is not so much that the young people do not know, as that they do not choose. There is something irreverent in the speculation, but perhaps the want of power has more to do with the wise resolutions of age than we are always willing to admit. It would be an instructive experiment to make an old man young again and leave him all his *savoir*. I scarcely think he would put his money in the Savings Bank after all; I doubt if he would be such an admirable son as we are led to expect; and as for his conduct in love, I believe firmly he would out-Herod Herod, and put the whole of his new compeers to the blush. Prudence is a wooden Juggernaut, before whom Benjamin Franklin walks with the portly air of a high-priest, and after whom dances many a successful merchant in the character of Atys. But it is not a deity to cultivate in youth. If a man lives to any considerable age, it cannot be denied that he laments his imprudences, but I notice he often laments his youth a deal more bitterly and with a more genuine intonation.

It is customary to say that age should be considered, because it comes last. It seems just as much to the point, that youth comes first. And the scale fairly kicks the beam, if you go on to add that age, in a majority of cases, never comes at all. Disease and accident make short work of even the most prosperous persons; death costs nothing, and the expense of a headstone is an inconsiderable trifle to the happy heir To be suddenly snuffed out in the middle of ambitious schemes is tragical enough at best; but when a man has been grudging himself his own life in the meanwhile, and saving up everything for the festival that was never to be, it becomes that hysterically moving sort of tragedy which lies on the confines of farce. The victim is dead—and he has cunningly overreached himself: a combination of calamities none the less absurd for being grim. To husband a favourite claret until the batch turns sour, is not at all an artful stroke of policy; and how much more with a whole cellar—

a whole bodily existence! People may lay down their lives with cheerfulness in the sure expectation of a blessed immortality; but that is a different affair from giving up youth with all its admirable pleasures, in the hope of a better quality of gruel in a more than problematical, nay, more than improbable, old age. We should not compliment a hungry man, who should refuse a whole dinner and reserve all his appetite for the dessert, before he knew whether there was to be any dessert or not. If there be such a thing as imprudence in the world, we surely have it here. We sail in leaky bottoms and on great and perilous waters; and to take a cue from the dolorous old naval ballad, we have heard the mermaidens singing, and know that we shall never see dry land any more. Old and young, we are all on our last cruise. If there is a fill of tobacco among the crew, for God's sake pass it round, and let us have a pipe before we go!

Indeed, by the report of our elders, this nervous preparation for old age is only trouble thrown away. We fall on guard, and after all it is a friend who comes to meet us. After the sun is down and the west faded, the heavens begin to fill with shining stars. So, as we grow old, a sort of equable jog-trot of feeling is substituted for the violent ups and downs of passion and disgust; the same influence that restrains our hopes, quiets our apprehensions; if the pleasures are less intense, the troubles are milder and more tolerable; and in a word, this period for which we are asked to hoard up everything as for a time of famine, is, in its own right, the richest, easiest, and happiest of life. Nay, by managing its own work and following its own happy inspiration, youth is doing the best it can to endow the leisure of age. A full, busy youth is your only prelude to a self-contained and independent age; and the muff inevitably develops into the bore. There are not many Doctor Johnsons, to set forth upon their first romantic voyage at sixty-four. If we wish to scale Mont Blanc or visit a thieves' kitchen in the East End, to go down in a diving-dress or up in a balloon, we must be about it while we are still young. It will not do to delay until we are clogged with prudence and limping with rheumatism, and people begin to ask us: "What does Gravity out of bed?" Youth is the time to go flashing from one end of the world to the other both in mind and body; to try the manners of different nations; to hear the chimes at midnight; to see sunrise in town and country; to be converted at a revival; to circumnavigate the metaphysics, write halting verses, run a mile to see a fire, and wait all day long in the theatre to applaud *Hernani*. There is some meaning in the old theory about wild oats; and a man who has not had his green-sickness and got done with it for good, is as little to be depended on as an unvaccinated infant. "It is extraordinary," said Lord Beaconsfield, one of the brightest and best preserved of youths up to the date of his last novel,[1] "it is extraordinary how hourly and how violently change the feelings of an unexperienced young man." And this mobility is a special talent entrusted to his care; a sort of indestructible virginity; a magic armour, with which he can pass unhurt through great dangers and come unbedaubed out of the miriest passages. Let him voyage, speculate, see all that he can, do all that he may; his soul has as many lives as a cat; he will live in all weathers, and never be a halfpenny the worse. Those who go to the devil in youth, with anything like

[1] *Lothair.*

a fair chance, were probably little worth saving from the first; they must have been feeble fellows—creatures made of putty and pack-thread, without steel or fire, anger or true joyfulness, in their composition; we may sympathise with their parents, but there is not much cause to go into mourning for themselves; for to be quite honest, the weak brother is the worst of mankind.

When the old man waggles his head and says, "Ah, so I thought when I was your age," he has proved the youth's case. Doubtless, whether from growth of experience or decline of animal heat, he thinks so no longer; but he thought so while he was young; and all men have thought so while they were young, since there was dew in the morning or hawthorn in May; and here is another young man adding his vote to those of previous generations and rivetting another link to the chain of testimony. It is as natural and as right for a young man to be imprudent and exaggerated, to live in swoops and circles, and beat about his cage like any other wild thing newly captured, as it is for old men to turn gray, or mothers to love their offspring, or heroes to die for something worthier than their lives.

By way of an apologue for the aged, when they feel more than usually tempted to offer their advice, let me recommend the following little tale. A child who had been remarkably fond of toys (and in particular of lead soldiers) found himself growing to the level of acknowledged boyhood without any abatement of this childish taste. He was thirteen; already he had been taunted for dallying overlong about the playbox; he had to blush if he was found among his lead soldiers; the shades of the prison-house were closing about him with a vengeance. There is nothing more difficult than to put the thoughts of children into the language of their elders; but this is the effect of his meditations at this juncture: "Plainly," he said, "I must give up my playthings in the meanwhile, since I am not in a position to secure myself against idle jeers. At the same time, I am sure that playthings are the very pick of life; all people give them up out of the same pusillanimous respect for those who are a little older; and if they do not return to them as soon as they can, it is only because they grow stupid and forget. I shall be wiser; I shall conform for a little to the ways of their foolish world; but so soon as I have made enough money, I shall retire and shut myself up among my playthings until the day I die." Nay, as he was passing in the train along the Esterel mountains between Cannes and Fréjus, he remarked a pretty house in an orange garden at the angle of a bay, and decided that this should be his Happy Valley. Astrea Redux; childhood was to come again! The idea has an air of simple nobility to me, not unworthy of Cincinnatus. And yet, as the reader has probably anticipated, it is never likely to be carried into effect. There was a worm i' the bud, a fatal error in the premises. Childhood must pass away, and then youth, as surely as age approaches. The true wisdom is to be always seasonable, and to change with a good grace in changing circumstances. To love playthings well as a child, to lead an adventurous and honourable youth, and to settle when the time arrives, into a green and smiling age, is to be a good artist in life and deserve well of yourself and your neighbour.

You need repent none of your youthful vagaries. They may have been over the score on one side, just as those of age are probably over the score on the other.

But they had a point; they not only befitted your age and expressed its attitude and passions, but they had a relation to what was outside of you, and implied criticisms on the existing state of things, which you need not allow to have been undeserved, because you now see that they were partial. All error, not merely verbal, is a strong way of stating that the current truth is incomplete. The follies of youth have a basis in sound reason, just as much as the embarrassing questions put by babes and sucklings. Their most anti-social acts indicate the defects of our society. When the torrent sweeps the man against a boulder, you must expect him to scream, and you need not be surprised if the scream is sometimes a theory. Shelley, chafing at the Church of England, discovered the cure of all evils in universal atheism. Generous lads irritated at the injustices of society, see nothing for it but the abolishment of everything and Kingdom Come of anarchy. Shelley was a young fool; so are these cock-sparrow revolutionaries. But it is better to be a fool than to be dead. It is better to emit a scream in the shape of a theory than to be entirely insensible to the jars and incongruities of life and take everything as it comes in a forlorn stupidity. Some people swallow the universe like a pill; they travel on through the world, like smiling images pushed from behind. For God's sake give me the young man who has brains enough to make a fool of himself! As for the others, the irony of facts shall take it out of their hands, and make fools of them in downright earnest, ere the farce be over. There shall be such a mopping and a mowing at the last day, and such blushing and confusion of countenance for all those who have been wise in their own esteem, and have not learnt the rough lessons that youth hands on to age.

If we are indeed here to perfect and complete our own natures, and grow larger, stronger, and more sympathetic against some nobler career in the future, we had all best bestir ourselves to the utmost while we have the time. To equip a dull, respectable person with wings would be but to make a parody of an angel.

In short, if youth is not quite right in its opinions, there is a strong probability that age is not much more so. Undying hope is co-ruler of the human bosom with infallible credulity. A man finds he has been wrong at every preceding stage of his career, only to deduce the astonishing conclusion that he is at last entirely right. Mankind, after centuries of failure, are still upon the eve of a thoroughly constitutional millennium. Since we have explored the maze so long without result, it follows, for poor human reason, that we cannot have to explore much longer; close by must be the centre, with a champagne luncheon and a piece of ornamental water. How if there were no centre at all, but just one alley after another, and the whole world a labyrinth without end or issue?

I overheard the other day a scrap of conversation, which I take the liberty to reproduce. "What I advance is true," said one. "But not the whole truth," answered the other. "Sir," returned the first (and it seemed to me there was a smack of Dr. Johnson in the speech), "Sir, there is no such thing as the whole truth!" Indeed, there is nothing so evident in life as that there are two sides to a question. History is one long illustration. The forces of nature are engaged, day by day, in cudgelling it into our backward intelligences. We never pause for a moment's consideration, but we admit it as an axiom. An enthusiast sways humanity exactly by disregarding this great truth, and dinning it into our ears that this or that question has only one possible solution; and your enthusiast is a fine florid fellow, dominates things for a while and shakes the world out of a doze; but when once he is gone, an army of quiet and uninfluential people set to work to remind us of the other side and demolish the generous imposture. While Calvin is putting everybody exactly right in his *Institutes*, and hot-headed Knox is thundering in the pulpit, Montaigne is already looking at the other side in his library in Perigord, and predicting that they will find as much to quarrel about in the Bible as they had found already in the Church. Age may have one side, but assuredly Youth has the other. There is nothing more certain than that both are right, except perhaps that both are wrong. Let them agree to differ; for who knows but what agreeing to differ may not be a form of agreement rather than a form of difference?

I suppose it is written that any one who sets up for a bit of a philosopher, must contradict himself to his very face. For here have I fairly talked myself into thinking that we have the whole thing before us at last; that there is no answer to the mystery, except that there are as many as you please; that there is no centre to the maze because, like the famous sphere, its centre is everywhere; and that agreeing to differ with every ceremony of politeness, is the only "one undisturbed song of pure concent" to which we are ever likely to lend our musical voices.

# AN APOLOGY FOR IDLERS

# AN APOLOGY FOR IDLERS

"BOSWELL: We grow weary when idle.

"JOHNSON: That is, sir, because others being busy, we want company; but if we were idle, there would be no growing weary; we should all entertain one another."

JUST now, when every one is bound, under pain of a decree in absence convicting them of *lèse*-respectability, to enter on some lucrative profession, and labour therein with something not far short of enthusiasm, a cry from the opposite party who are content when they have enough, and like to look on and enjoy in the meanwhile, savours a little of bravado and gasconade. And yet this should not be. Idleness so called, which does not consist in doing nothing, but in doing a great deal not recognised in the dogmatic formularies of the ruling class, has as good a right to state its position as industry itself. It is admitted that the presence of people who refuse to enter in the great handicap race for sixpenny pieces, is at once an insult and a disenchantment for those who do. A fine fellow (as we see so many) takes his determination, votes for the sixpences, and in the emphatic Americanism, "goes for" them. And while such an one is ploughing distressfully up the road, it is not hard to understand his resentment, when he perceives cool persons in the meadows by the wayside, lying with a handkerchief over their ears and a glass at their elbow. Alexander is touched in a very delicate place by the disregard of Diogenes. Where was the glory of having taken Rome for these tumultuous barbarians, who poured into the Senate house, and found the Fathers sitting silent and unmoved by their success? It is a sore thing to have laboured along and scaled the arduous hilltops, and when all is done, find humanity indifferent to your achievement. Hence physicists condemn the unphysical; financiers have only a superficial toleration for those who know little of stocks; literary persons despise the unlettered; and people of all pursuits combine to disparage those who have none.

But though this is one difficulty of the subject, it is not the greatest. You could not be put in prison for speaking against industry, but you can be sent to Coventry for speaking like a fool. The greatest difficulty with most subjects is to do them well; therefore, please to remember this is an apology. It is certain that much may be judiciously argued in favour of diligence; only there is something to be said against it, and that is what, on the present occasion, I have to say. To state one argument is not necessarily to be deaf to all others, and that a man has written a book of travels in Montenegro, is no reason why he should never have been to Richmond.

It is surely beyond a doubt that people should be a good deal idle in youth. For though here and there a Lord Macaulay may escape from school honours with all his wits about him, most boys pay so dear for their medals that they never afterwards have a shot in their locker, and begin the world bankrupt. And the same holds true during all the time a lad is educating himself, or suffering others to educate him. It must have been a very foolish old gentleman who addressed Johnson at

Oxford in these words: "Young man, ply your book diligently now, and acquire a stock of knowledge; for when years come upon you, you will find that poring upon books will be but an irksome task." The old gentleman seems to have been unaware that many other things besides reading grow irksome, and not a few become impossible, by the time a man has to use spectacles and cannot walk without a stick. Books are good enough in their own way, but they are a mighty bloodless substitute for life. It seems a pity to sit, like the Lady of Shalott, peering into a mirror, with your back turned on all the bustle and glamour of reality. And if a man reads very hard, as the old anecdote reminds us, he will have little time for thought.

If you look back on your own education, I am sure it will not be the full, vivid, instructive hours of truantry that you regret; you would rather cancel some lack-lustre periods between sleep and waking in the class. For my own part, I have attended a good many lectures in my time. I still remember that the spinning of a top is a case of Kinetic Stability. I still remember that Emphyteusis is not a disease, nor Stillicide a crime. But though I would not willingly part with such scraps of science, I do not set the same store by them as by certain other odds and ends that I came by in the open street while I was playing truant. This is not the moment to dilate on that mighty place of education, which was the favourite school of Dickens and of Balzac, and turns out yearly many inglorious masters in the Science of the Aspects of Life. Suffice it to say this: if a lad does not learn in the streets, it is because he has no faculty of learning Nor is the truant always in the streets, for if he prefers he may go out by the gardened suburbs into the country

He may pitch on some tuft of lilacs over a burn, and smoke innumerable pipes to the tune of the water on the stones. A bird will sing in the thicket. And there he may fall into a vein of kindly thought, and see things in a new perspective. Why, if this be not education, what is? We may conceive Mr. Worldly Wiseman accosting such an one, and the conversation that should thereupon ensue:—

"How now, young fellow, what dost thou here?"

"Truly, sir, I take mine ease."

"Is not this the hour of the class? and should'st thou not be plying thy Book with diligence, to the end thou mayest obtain knowledge?"

"Nay, but thus also I follow after Learning, by your leave."

"Learning, quotha! After what fashion, I pray thee? Is it mathematics?"

"No, to be sure."

"Is it metaphysics?"

"Nor that."

"Is it some language?"

"Nay, it is no language."

"Is it a trade?"

"Nor a trade neither."

"Why, then, what is't?"

"Indeed, sir, as a time may soon come for me to go upon Pilgrimage, I am desirous to note what is commonly done by persons in my case, and where are the ugliest Sloughs and Thickets on the Road; as also, what manner of Staff is of the best service. Moreover, I lie here, by this water, to learn by root-of-heart a lesson which my master teaches me to call Peace, or Contentment."

Hereupon Mr. Worldly Wiseman was much commoved with passion, and shaking his cane with a very threatful countenance, broke forth upon this wise: "Learning, quotha!" said he; "I would have all such rogues scourged by the Hangman!"

And so he would go his way, ruffling out his cravat with a crackle of starch, like a turkey when it spread its feathers.

Now this, of Mr. Wiseman's, is the common opinion. A fact is not called a fact, but a piece of gossip, if it does not fall into one of your scholastic categories. An inquiry must be in some acknowledged direction, with a name to go by; or else you are not inquiring at all, only lounging; and the workhouse is too good for you. It is supposed that all knowledge is at the bottom of a well, or the far end of a telescope. Sainte-Beuve, as he grew older, came to regard all experience as a single great book, in which to study for a few years ere we go hence; and it seemed all one to him whether you should read in Chapter xx., which is the differential calculus, or in Chapter xxxix., which is hearing the band play in the gardens. As a matter of fact, an intelligent person, looking out of his eyes and hearkening in his ears, with a smile on his face all the time, will get more true education than many another in a life of heroic vigils. There is certainly some chill and arid knowledge to be found upon the summits of formal and laborious science: but it is all round about you, and for the trouble of looking, that you will acquire the warm and palpitating facts of life. While others are filling their memory with a lumber of words, one-half of which they will forget before the week be out, your truant may learn some really useful art: to play the fiddle, to know a good cigar, or to speak with ease and opportunity to all varieties of men.

Many who have "plied their book diligently," and know all about some one branch or another of accepted lore, come out of the study with an ancient and owl-like demeanour, and prove dry, stockish, and dyspeptic in all the better and brighter parts of life. Many make a large fortune, who remain under-bred and pathetically stupid to the last. And meanwhile there goes the idler, who began life along with them—by your leave, a different picture. He has had time to take care of his health and his spirits; he has been a great deal in the open air, which is the most salutary of all things for both body and mind; and if he has never read the great Book in very recondite places, he has dipped into it and skimmed it over to excellent purpose. Might not the student afford some Hebrew roots, and the business man some of his half-crowns, for a share of the idler's knowledge of life at large, and Art of Living? Nay, and the idler has another and more important quality than these. I mean his wisdom. He who has much looked on at the childish satisfaction of other people in their hobbies, will regard his own with only a very ironical indulgence. He will not be heard among the dogmatists. He will have a great and cool allowance for all sorts of people and opinions. If he finds no out-of-the-way truths, he will identify himself with no very burning falsehood. His way takes him along a by-road, not much frequented, but very even and pleasant, which is called Commonplace Lane, and leads to the Belvedere of Common-sense. Thence he shall command an agreeable, if no very noble prospect; and while others behold the East and West, the Devil and the Sunrise, he will be contentedly aware of a sort of morning hour upon all sublunary things, with an army of shadows running speedily and in many different directions into the great daylight of Eternity. The shadows and the generations, the shrill doctors and the plangent wars, go by into ultimate silence and emptiness; but underneath all this, a man may see, out of the Belvedere windows, much green and peaceful landscape; many fire-lit parlours; good people laughing, drinking, and making love as they did before the Flood or the French Revolution; and the old shepherd telling his tale under the hawthorn.

Extreme *busyness*, whether at school or college, kirk or market, is a symptom of deficient vitality; and a faculty for idleness implies a catholic appetite and a strong sense of personal identity. There is a sort of dead-alive, hackneyed people about, who are scarcely conscious of living except in the exercise of some conventional occupation. Bring these fellows into the country or set them aboard ship, and you will see how they pine for their desk or their study. They have no curiosity; they cannot give themselves over to random provocations; they do not take pleasure in the exercise of their faculties for its own sake; and unless Necessity lays about them with a stick, they will even stand still. It is no good speaking to such folk: they *cannot* be idle, their nature is not generous enough; and they pass those hours in a sort of coma, which are not dedicated to furious moiling in the gold-mill. When they do not require to go to the office, when they are not hungry and have no mind to drink, the whole breathing world is a blank to them. If they have to wait an hour or so for a train, they fall into a stupid trance with their eyes open. To see them, you would suppose there was nothing to look at and no one to speak with; you would imagine they were paralysed or alienated; and yet very possibly they are hard workers in their own way, and have good eyesight for a flaw in a deed or a turn of the market. They have been to school and college, but all the time they had their eye on the medal; they have gone about in the world and mixed with clever people, but all the time they were thinking of their own affairs. As if a man's soul were not too small to begin with, they have dwarfed and narrowed theirs by a life of all work and no play; until here they are at forty, with a listless attention, a mind vacant of all material of amusement, and not one thought to rub against another, while they wait for the train. Before he was breeched, he might have clambered on the boxes; when he was twenty, he would have stared at the girls; but now the pipe is smoked out, the snuff-box empty, and my gentleman sits bolt upright upon a bench, with lamentable eyes. This does not appeal to me as being Success in Life.

But it is not only the person himself who suffers from his busy habits, but his wife and children, his friends and relations, and down to the very people he sits with in a railway-carriage or an omnibus. Perpetual devotion to what a man calls his business, is only to be sustained by perpetual neglect of many other things. And it is not by any means certain that a man's business is the most important thing he has to do. To an impartial estimate it will seem clear that many of the wisest, most virtuous, and most beneficent parts that are to be played upon the Theatre of Life are filled by gratuitous performers, and pass, among the world at large, as phases of idleness. For in that Theatre, not only the walking gentlemen, singing chambermaids, and diligent fiddlers in the orchestra, but those who look on and clap their hands from the benches, do really play a part and fulfil important offices towards the general result. You are no doubt very dependent on the care of your lawyer and stockbroker, of the guards and signalmen who convey you rapidly from place to place, and the policemen who walk the streets for your protection; but is there not a thought of gratitude in your heart for certain other benefactors who set you smiling when they fall in your way, or season your dinner with good company? Colonel Newcome helped to lose his friend's money; Fred Bayham had an ugly trick of borrowing shirts; and yet they were better people to fall among than Mr. Barnes. And though Falstaff was neither sober nor very honest, I think I could name one or two long-faced Barabbases whom the world could better have done without. Hazlitt mentions that he was more sensible of obligation to Northcote, who had never done him anything he could call a service, than to his whole circle of ostentatious friends; for he thought a good companion emphatically the greatest benefactor. I know there are people in the world who cannot feel grateful unless the favour has been done them at the cost of pain and difficulty. But this is a churlish disposition. A man may send you six sheets of letter-paper covered with the most entertaining gossip, or you may pass half-an-hour pleasantly, perhaps profitably, over an article of his; do you think the service would be greater, if he had made the manuscript in his heart's blood, like a compact with the devil? Do you really fancy you should be more beholden to your correspondent, if he had been damning you all the while for your importunity? Pleasures are more beneficial than duties because, like the quality of mercy, they are not strained, and they are twice blest. There must always be two to a kiss, and there may be a score in a jest; but wherever there is an element of sacrifice, the favour is conferred with pain, and, among generous people, received with confusion. There is no duty we so much underrate as the duty of being happy. By being happy, we sow anonymous benefits upon the world, which remain unknown even to ourselves, or when they are disclosed, surprise nobody so much as the benefactor. The other day, a ragged, barefoot boy ran down the street after a marble, with so jolly an air that he set every one he passed into a good humour; one of these persons, who had been delivered from more than usually black thoughts, stopped the little fellow and gave him some money with this remark: "You see what sometimes comes of looking pleased." If he had looked pleased before, he had now to look both pleased and mystified. For my part, I justify this encouragement of smiling rather than tearful children; I do not wish to pay for tears anywhere but upon the stage; but I am prepared to deal largely in the opposite commodity. A happy man or woman is a better thing to find than a five-pound note. He or she is a radiating focus of goodwill; and their entrance into a room is as though another candle had been lighted. We need not care whether they could prove the forty-seventh proposition; they do a better thing than that, they practically demonstrate the great Theorem of the Liveableness of Life. Consequently, if a person cannot be happy without remaining idle, idle he should remain. It is a revolutionary precept; but thanks to hunger and the workhouse, one not easily to be abused; and within practical limits, it is one of the most incontestable truths in the whole Body of Morality. Look at one of your industrious fellows for a moment, I beseech you. He sows hurry and reaps indigestion; he puts a vast deal of activity out to interest, and receives a large measure of nervous derangement in return. Either he absents himself entirely from all fellowship, and lives a recluse in a garret, with carpet slippers and a leaden inkpot; or he comes among people swiftly and bitterly, in a contraction of his whole nervous system, to discharge some temper before he returns to work. I do not care how much or how well he works, this fellow is an evil feature in other people's lives. They would be happier if he were dead. They could easier do without his services in the Circumlocution Office, than they can tolerate his fractious spirits. He poisons life at the well-head. It is better to be beggared out of hand by a scapegrace nephew, than daily hag-ridden by a peevish uncle.

And what, in God's name, is all this pother about? For what cause do they embitter their own and other people's lives? That a man should publish three or thirty articles a year, that he should finish or not finish his great allegorical picture, are questions of little interest to the world. The ranks of life are full; and although a thousand fall, there are always some to go into the breach. When they told Joan of Arc she should be at home minding women's work, she answered there were plenty to spin and wash. And so, even with your own rare gifts! When nature is "so careless of the single life," why should we coddle ourselves into the fancy that our own is of exceptional importance? Suppose Shakespeare had been knocked on the head some dark night in Sir Thomas Lucy's preserves, the world would have wagged on better or worse, the pitcher gone to the well, the scythe to the corn, and the student to his book; and no one been any the wiser of the loss. There are not many works extant, if you look the alternative all over, which are worth the price of a pound of tobacco to a man of limited means. This is a sobering reflection for the proudest of our earthly vanities. Even a tobacconist may, upon consideration, find no great cause for personal vainglory in the phrase; for although tobacco is an admirable sedative, the qualities necessary for retailing it are neither rare nor precious in themselves. Alas and alas! you may take it how you will, but the services of no single individual are indispensable. Atlas was just a gentleman with a protracted nightmare! And yet you see merchants who go and labour themselves into a great fortune and thence into the bankruptcy court; scribblers who keep scribbling at little articles until their temper is a cross to all who come about them, as though Pharaoh should set the Israelites to make a pin instead of a pyramid: and fine young men who work themselves into a decline, and are driven off in a hearse with white plumes upon it. Would you not suppose these persons had been whispered, by the Master of the Ceremonies, the promise of some momentous destiny? and that this lukewarm bullet on which they play their farces was the bull's-eye and centre-point of all the universe? And yet it is not so. The ends for which they give away their priceless youth, for all they know, may be chimerical or hurtful; the glory and riches they expect may never come, or may find them indifferent; and they and the world they inhabit are so inconsiderable that the mind freezes at the thought.

# ORDERED SOUTH

# ORDERED SOUTH

By a curious irony of fate, the places to which we are sent when health deserts us are often singularly beautiful. Often, too, they are places we have visited in former years, or seen briefly in passing by, and kept ever afterwards in pious memory; and we please ourselves with the fancy that we shall repeat many vivid and pleasurable sensations, and take up again the thread of our enjoyment in the same spirit as we let it fall. We shall now have an opportunity of finishing many pleasant excursions, interrupted of yore before our curiosity was fully satisfied. It may be that we have kept in mind, during all these years, the recollection of some valley into which we have just looked down for a moment before we lost sight of it in the disorder of the hills; it may be that we have lain awake at night, and agreeably tantalised ourselves with the thought of corners we had never turned, or summits we had all but climbed: we shall now be able, as we tell ourselves, to complete all these unfinished pleasures, and pass beyond the barriers that confined our recollections.

The promise is so great, and we are all so easily led away when hope and memory are both in one story, that I daresay the sick man is not very inconsolable when he receives sentence of banishment, and is inclined to regard his ill-health as not the least fortunate accident of his life. Nor is he immediately undeceived. The stir and speed of the journey, and the restlessness that goes to bed with him as he tries to sleep between two days of noisy progress, fever him, and stimulate his dull nerves into something of their old quickness and sensibility. And so he can enjoy the faint autumnal splendour of the landscape, as he sees hill and plain, vineyard and forest, clad in one wonderful glory of fairy gold, which the first great winds of winter will transmute, as in the fable, into withered leaves. And so too he can enjoy the admirable brevity and simplicity of such little glimpses of country and country ways as flash upon him through the windows of the train; little glimpses that have a character all their own; sights seen as a travelling swallow might see them from the wing, or Iris as she went abroad over the land on some Olympian errand. Here and there, indeed, a few children huzzah and wave their hands to the express; but for the most part, it is an interruption too brief and isolated to attract much notice; the sheep do not cease from browsing; a girl sits balanced on the projecting tiller of a canal boat, so precariously that it seems as if a fly or the splash of a leaping fish would be enough to overthrow the dainty equilibrium, and yet all these hundreds of tons of coal and wood and iron have been precipitated roaring past her very ear, and there is not a start, not a tremor, not a turn of the averted head, to indicate that she has been even conscious of its passage. Herein, I think, lies the chief attraction of railway travel. The speed is so easy, and the train disturbs so little the scenes through which it takes us, that our heart becomes full of the placidity and stillness of the country; and while the body is borne forward in the flying chain of carriages, the thoughts alight, as the humour moves them, at unfrequented stations; they make haste up the poplar alley that leads toward the town; they are left behind with the signalman as, shading his eyes with his hand, he watches the long train sweep away into the golden distance.

Moreover, there is still before the invalid the shock of wonder and delight with which he will learn that he has passed the indefinable line that separates South from North. And this is an uncertain moment; for sometimes the consciousness is forced upon him early, on the occasion of some slight association, a colour, a flower, or a scent; and sometimes not until, one fine morning, he wakes up with the southern sunshine peeping through the *persiennes*, and the southern patois confusedly audible below the windows. Whether it come early or late, however, this pleasure will not end with the anticipation, as do so many others of the same family. It will leave him wider awake than it found him, and give a new significance to all he may see for many days to come. There is something in the mere name of the South that carries enthusiasm along with it. At the sound of the word, he pricks up his ears; he becomes as anxious to seek out beauties and to get by heart the permanent lines and character of the landscape, as if he had been told that it was all his own—an estate out of which he had been kept unjustly, and which he was now to receive in free and full possession. Even those who have never been there before feel as if they had been; and everybody goes comparing, and seeking for the familiar, and finding it with such ecstasies of recognition, that one would think they were coming home after a weary absence, instead of travelling hourly farther abroad.

It is only after he is fairly arrived and settled down in his chosen corner, that the invalid begins to understand the change that has befallen him. Everything about him is as he had remembered, or as he had anticipated. Here, at his feet, under his eyes, are the olive gardens and the blue sea. Nothing can change the eternal magnificence of form of the naked Alps behind Mentone; nothing, not even the crude curves of the railway, can utterly deform the suavity of contour of one bay after another along the whole reach of the Riviera. And of all this, he has only a cold head-knowledge that is divorced from enjoyment. He recognises with his intelligence that this thing and that thing is beautiful, while in his heart of hearts he has to confess that it is not beautiful for him. It is in vain that he spurs his discouraged spirit; in vain that he chooses out points of view, and stands there, looking with all his eyes, and waiting for some return of the pleasure that he remembers in other days, as the sick folk may have awaited the coming of the angel at the pool of Bethesda. He is like an enthusiast leading about with him a stolid, indifferent tourist. There is some one by who is out of sympathy with the scene, and is not moved up to the measure of the occasion; and that some one is himself. The world is disenchanted for him. He seems to himself to touch things with muffled hands, and to see them through a veil. His life becomes a palsied fumbling after notes that are silent when he has found and struck them. He cannot recognise that this phlegmatic and unimpressionable body with which he now goes burthened, is the same that he knew heretofore so quick and delicate and alive.

He is tempted to lay the blame on the very softness and amenity of the climate, and to fancy that in the rigours of the winter at home, these dead emotions would revive and flourish. A longing for the brightness and silence of fallen snow seizes him at such times. He is homesick for the hale rough weather; for the tracery of the frost upon his window-panes at morning, the reluctant descent of the first flakes, and the white roofs relieved against the sombre sky. And yet the stuff of which these yearnings are made, is of the flimsiest: if but the thermometer fall a little below its ordinary Mediterranean level, or a wind come down from the snow-clad Alps behind, the spirit of his fancies changes upon the instant, and many a doleful vignette of the grim wintry streets at home returns to him, and begins to haunt his memory. The hopeless, huddled attitude of tramps in doorways; the flinching gait of barefoot children on the icy pavement; the sheen of the rainy streets towards afternoon; the meagre anatomy of the poor defined by the clinging of wet garments; the high canorous note of the North-easter on days when the very houses seem to stiffen with cold: these, and such as these, crowd back upon him, and mockingly substitute themselves for the fanciful winter scenes with which he had pleased himself a while before. He cannot be glad enough that he is where he is. If only the others could be there also; if only those tramps could lie down for a little in the sunshine, and those children warm their feet, this once, upon a kindlier earth; if only there were no cold anywhere, and no nakedness, and no hunger; if only it were as well with all men as it is with him!

For it is not altogether ill with the invalid, after all. If it is only rarely that anything penetrates vividly into his numbed spirit, yet, when anything does, it brings with it a joy that is all the more poignant for its very rarity. There is something pathetic in these occasional returns of a glad activity of heart. In his lowest hours he will be stirred and awakened by many such; and they will spring perhaps from very trivial sources; as a friend once said to me, the "spirit of delight" comes often on small wings. For the pleasure that we take in beautiful nature is essentially capricious. It comes sometimes when we least look for it; and sometimes, when we expect it most certainly, it leaves us to gape joylessly for days together, in the very home-land of the beautiful. We may have passed a place a thousand times and one; and on the thousand and second it will be transfigured, and stand forth in a certain splendour of reality from the dull circle of surroundings; so that we see it "with a child's first pleasure," as Wordsworth saw the daffodils by the lake side. And if this falls out capriciously with the healthy, how much more so with the invalid. Some day he will find his first violet, and be lost in pleasant wonder, by what alchemy the cold earth of the clods, and the vapid air and rain, can be transmuted into colour so rich and odour so touchingly sweet. Or perhaps he may see a group of washerwomen relieved, on a spit of shingle, against the blue sea, or a meeting of flower-gatherers in the tempered daylight of an olive-garden; and something significant or monumental in the grouping, something in the harmony of faint colour that is always characteristic of the dress of these southern women, will come home to him unexpectedly, and awake in him that satisfaction with which we tell ourselves that we are the richer by one more beautiful experience. Or it may be something even slighter: as when the opulence of the sunshine, which somehow gets lost and fails to produce its effect on the large scale, is suddenly revealed to him by the chance isolation—as he changes the position of his sunshade—of a yard or two of roadway with its stones and weeds.

And then, there is no end to the infinite variety of the olive-yards themselves. Even the colour is indeterminate and continually shifting: now you would say it was green, now gray, now blue; now tree stands above tree, like "cloud on cloud," massed into filmy indistinctness; and now, at the wind's will, the whole sea of foliage is shaken and broken up with little momentary silverings and shadows. But every one sees the world in his own way. To some the glad moment may have arrived on other provocations; and their recollection may be most vivid of the stately gait of women carrying burthens on their heads; of tropical effects, with canes and naked rock and sunlight; of the relief of cypresses; of the troubled, busy-looking groups of sea-pines, that seem always as if they were being wielded and swept together by a whirlwind; of the air coming, laden with virginal perfumes, over the myrtles and the scented underwood; of the empurpled hills standing up, solemn and sharp, out of the green-gold air of the east at evening.

There go many elements, without doubt, to the making of one such moment of intense perception; and it is on the happy agreement of these many elements, on the harmonious vibration of many nerves, that the whole delight of the moment must depend. Who can forget how, when he has chanced upon some attitude of complete restfulness, after long uneasy rolling to and fro on grass or heather, the whole fashion of the landscape has been changed for him, as though the sun had just broken forth, or a great artist had only then completed, by some cunning touch, the composition of the picture? And not only a change of posture—a snatch of perfume, the sudden singing of a bird, the freshness of some pulse of air from an invisible sea, the light shadow of a travelling cloud, the merest nothing that sends a little shiver along the most infinitesimal nerve of a man's body —not one of the least of these but has a hand somehow in the general effect, and brings some refinement of its own into the character of the pleasure we feel.

And if the external conditions are thus varied and subtle, even more so are those within our own bodies. No man can find out the world, says Solomon, from beginning to end, because the world is in his heart; and so it is impossible for any of us to understand, from beginning to end, that agreement of harmonious circumstances that creates in us the highest pleasure of admiration, precisely because some of these circumstances are hidden from us for ever in the constitution of our own bodies. After we have reckoned up all that we can see or hear or feel, there still remains to be taken into account some sensibility more delicate than usual in the nerves affected, or some exquisite refinement in the architecture of the brain, which is indeed to the sense of the beautiful as the eye or the ear to the sense of hearing or sight. We admire splendid views and great pictures; and yet what is truly admirable is rather the mind within us, that gathers together these scattered details for its delight, and makes out of certain colours, certain distributions of graduated light and darkness, that intelligible whole which alone we call a picture or a view. Hazlitt, relating in one of his essays how he went on foot from one great man's house to another's in search of works of art, begins suddenly to triumph over these noble and wealthy owners, because he was more capable of enjoying their costly possessions than they were; because they had paid the money and he had received the pleasure. And the occasion is a fair one for self-complacency. While the one man was working to be able to buy the picture, the other was working to be able to enjoy the picture. An inherited aptitude will have been diligently improved in either case; only the one man has made for himself a fortune, and the other has made for himself a living spirit. It is a fair occasion for self-complacency, I repeat, when the event shows a man to have chosen the better part, and laid out his life more wisely, in the long run, than those who have credit for most wisdom. And yet even this is not a good unmixed; and like all other possessions, although in a less degree, the possession of a brain that has been thus improved and cultivated, and made into the prime organ of a man's enjoyment, brings with it certain inevitable cares and disappointments. The happiness of such an one comes to depend greatly upon those fine shades of sensation that heighten and harmonise the coarser elements of beauty. And thus a degree of nervous prostration, that to other men would be hardly disagreeable, is enough to overthrow for him the whole fabric of his life, to take, except at rare moments, the edge off his pleasures, and to meet him wherever he goes with failure, and the sense of want, and disenchantment of the world and life.

It is not in such numbness of spirit only that the life of the invalid resembles a premature old age. Those excursions that he had promised himself to finish, prove too long or too arduous for his feeble body; and the barrier-hills are as impassable as ever. Many a white town that sits far out on the promontory, many a comely fold of wood on the mountain-side, beckons and allures his imagination day after day, and is yet as inaccessible to his feet as the clefts and gorges of the clouds. The sense of distance grows upon him wonderfully; and after some feverish efforts and the fretful uneasiness of the first few days, he falls contentedly in with the restrictions of his weakness. His narrow round becomes pleasant and familiar to him as the cell to a contented prisoner. Just as he has fallen already out of the mid race of active life, he now falls out of the little eddy that circulates in the shallow waters of the sanatorium. He sees the country people come and go about their every-day affairs, the foreigners stream out in goodly pleasure parties; the stir of man's activity is all about him, as he suns himself inertly in some sheltered corner; and he looks on with a patriarchal impersonality of interest, such as a man may feel when he pictures to himself the fortunes of his remote descendants, or the robust old age of the oak he has planted over-night.

In this falling aside, in this quietude and desertion of other men, there is no inharmonious prelude to the last quietude and desertion of the grave; in this dulness of the senses there is a gentle preparation for the final insensibility of death. And to him the idea of mortality comes in a shape less violent and harsh than is its wont, less as an abrupt catastrophe than as a thing of infinitesimal gradation, and the last step on a long decline of way. As we turn to and fro in bed, and every moment the movements grow feebler and smaller and the attitude more restful and easy, until sleep overtakes us at a stride and we move no more, so desire after desire leaves him; day by day his strength decreases, and the circle of his activity grows ever narrower; and he feels, if he is to be thus tenderly weaned from the passion of life, thus gradually inducted into the slumber of death, that when at last the end comes, it will come quietly and fitly. If anything is to reconcile poor spirits to the coming of the last enemy, surely it should be such a mild approach as this; not to hale us forth with violence, but to persuade us from a place we have no further pleasure in. It is not so much, indeed, death that approaches as life that withdraws and withers up from round about him. He has outlived his own usefulness, and almost his own enjoyment; and if there is to be no recovery; if never again will he be young and strong and passionate, if the actual present shall be to him always like a thing read in a book or remembered out of the far-away past; if, in fact, this be veritably nightfall, he will not wish greatly for the continuance of a twilight that only strains and disappoints the eyes, but steadfastly await the perfect darkness. He will pray for Medea: when she comes, let her either rejuvenate or slay.

And yet the ties that still attach him to the world are many and kindly. The sight of children has a significance for him such as it may have for the aged also, but not for others. If he has been used to feel humanely, and to look upon life somewhat more widely than from the narrow loophole of personal pleasure and advancement, it is strange how small a portion of his thoughts will be changed or embittered by this proximity of death. He knows that already, in English counties, the sower follows the ploughman up the face of the field, and the rooks follow the sower; and he knows also that he may not live to go home again and see the corn spring and ripen, and be cut down at last, and brought home with gladness. And yet the future of this harvest, the continuance of drought or the coming of rain unseasonably, touch him as sensibly as ever. For he has long been used to wait with interest the issue of events in which his own concern was nothing; and to be joyful in a plenty, and sorrowful for a famine, that did not increase or diminish, by one half loaf, the equable sufficiency of his own supply. Thus there remain unaltered all the disinterested hopes for mankind and a better future which have been the solace and inspiration of his life. These he has set beyond the reach of any fate that only menaces himself; and it makes small difference whether he die five thousand years, or five thousand and fifty years, before the good epoch for which he faithfully labours. He has not deceived himself; he has known from the beginning that he followed the pillar of fire and cloud, only to perish himself in the wilderness, and that it was reserved for others to enter joyfully into possession of the land. And so, as everything grows grayer and quieter about him, and slopes towards extinction, these unfaded visions accompany his sad decline, and follow him, with friendly voices and hopeful words, into the very vestibule of death. The desire of love or of fame scarcely moved him, in his days of health, more strongly than these generous aspirations move him now; and so life is carried forward beyond life, and a vista kept open for the eyes of hope, even when his hands grope already on the face of the impassable.

Lastly, he is bound tenderly to life by the thought of his friends; or shall we not say rather, that by their thought for him, by their unchangeable solicitude and love, he remains woven into the very stuff of life, beyond the power of bodily dissolution to undo? In a thousand ways will he survive and be perpetuated. Much of Etienne de la Boetie survived during all the years in which Montaigne continued to converse with him on the pages of the ever-delightful essays. Much of what was truly Goethe was dead already when he revisited places that knew him no more, and found no better consolation than the promise of his own verses, that soon he too would be at rest. Indeed, when we think of what it is that we most seek and cherish, and find most pride and pleasure in calling ours, it will sometimes seem to us as if our friends, at our decease, would suffer loss more truly than ourselves. As a monarch who should care more for the outlying colonies he knows on the map or through the report of his vicegerents, than for the trunk of his empire under his eyes at home, are we not more concerned about the shadowy life that we have in the hearts of others, and that portion in their thoughts and fancies which, in a certain far-away sense, belongs to us, than about the real knot of our identity—that central metropolis of self, of which alone we are immediately aware—or the diligent service of arteries and veins and infinitesimal activity of ganglia, which we know (as we know a proposition in Euclid) to be the source and substance of the whole? At the death of every one whom we love, some fair and honourable portion of our existence falls away, and we are dislodged from one of these dear provinces; and they are not, perhaps, the most fortunate who survive a long series of such impoverishments, till their life and influence narrow gradually into the meagre limit of their own spirits, and death, when he comes at last, can destroy them at one blow.

NOTE.—To this essay I must in honesty append a word or two of qualification; for this is one of the points on which a slightly greater age teaches us a slightly different wisdom:

A youth delights in generalities, and keeps loose from particular obligations; he jogs on the footpath way, himself pursuing butterflies, but courteously lending his applause to the advance of the human species and the coming of the kingdom of justice and love. As he grows older, he begins to think more narrowly of man's action in the general, and perhaps more arrogantly of his own in the particular. He has not that same unspeakable trust in what he would have done had he been spared, seeing finally that that would have been little; but he has a far higher notion of the blank that he will make by dying. A young man feels himself one too many in the world; his is a painful situation; he has no calling; no obvious utility; no ties, but to his parents, and these he is sure to disregard. I do not think that a proper allowance has been made for this true cause of suffering in youth; but by the mere fact of a prolonged existence, we outgrow either the fact or else the feeling. Either we become so callously accustomed to our own useless figure in the world, or else—and this, thank God, in the majority of cases—we so collect about us the interest or the love of our fellows, so multiply our effective part in the affairs of life, that we need to entertain no longer the question of our right to be.

And so in the majority of cases, a man who fancies himself dying, will get cold comfort from the very youthful view expressed in this essay. He, as a living man, has some to help, some to love, some to correct; it may be, some to punish. These duties cling, not upon humanity, but upon the man himself. It is he, not another, who is one woman's son and a second woman's husband and a third woman's father. That life which began so small, has now grown, with a myriad filaments, into the lives of others. It is not indispensable; another will take the place and shoulder the discharged responsibility; but the better the man and the nobler his purposes, the more will he be tempted to regret the extinction of his powers and the deletion of his personality. To have lived a generation, is not only to have grown at home in that perplexing medium, but to have assumed innumerable duties. To die at such an age, has, for all but the entirely base, something of the air of a betrayal. A man does not only reflect upon what he might have done in a future that is never to be his; but beholding himself so early a deserter from the fight, he eats his heart for the good he might have done already. To have been so useless and now to lose all hope of being useful any more—there it is that death and memory assail him. And even if mankind shall go on, founding heroic cities, practising heroic virtues, rising steadily from strength to strength; even if his work shall be fulfilled, his friends consoled, his wife remarried by a better than he; how shall this alter, in one jot, his estimation of a career which was his only business in this world, which was so fitfully pursued, and which is now so ineffectively to end?

# ÆS TRIPLEX

## ÆS TRIPLEX

The changes wrought by death are in themselves so sharp and final, and so terrible and melancholy in their consequences, that the thing stands alone in man's experience, and has no parallel upon earth. It outdoes all other accidents because it is the last of them. Sometimes it leaps suddenly upon its victims, like a Thug; sometimes it lays a regular siege and creeps upon their citadel during a score of years. And when the business is done, there is sore havoc made in other people's lives, and a pin knocked out by which many subsidiary friendships hung together. There are empty chairs, solitary walks, and single beds at night. Again, in taking away our friends, death does not take them away utterly, but leaves behind a mocking, tragical, and soon intolerable residue, which must be hurriedly concealed. Hence a whole chapter of sights and customs striking to the mind, from the pyramids of Egypt to the gibbets and dule trees of mediæval Europe. The poorest persons have a bit of pageant going towards the tomb; memorial stones are set up over the least memorable; and, in order to preserve some show of respect for what remains of our old loves and friendships, we must accompany it with much grimly ludicrous ceremonial, and the hired undertaker parades before the door. All this, and much more of the same sort, accompanied by the eloquence of poets, has gone a great way to put humanity in error; nay, in many philosophies the error has been embodied and laid down with every circumstance of logic; although in real life the bustle and swiftness, in leaving people little time to think, have not left them time enough to go dangerously wrong in practice.

As a matter of fact, although few things are spoken of with more fearful whisperings than this prospect of death, few have less influence on conduct under healthy circumstances. We have all heard of cities in South America built upon the side of fiery mountains, and how, even in this tremendous neighbourhood, the inhabitants are not a jot more impressed by the solemnity of mortal conditions than if they were delving gardens in the greenest corner of England. There are serenades and suppers and much gallantry among the myrtles overhead; and meanwhile the foundation shudders underfoot, the bowels of the mountain growl, and at any moment living ruin may leap sky-high into the moonlight, and tumble man and his merry-making in the dust. In the eyes of very young people, and very dull old ones, there is something indescribably reckless and desperate in such a picture. It seems not credible that respectable married people, with umbrellas, should find appetite for a bit of supper within quite a long distance of a fiery mountain; ordinary life begins to smell of high-handed debauch when it is carried on so close to a catastrophe; and even cheese and salad, it seems, could hardly be relished in such circumstances without something like a defiance of the Creator. It should be a place for nobody but hermits dwelling in prayer and maceration, or mere born-devils drowning care in a perpetual carouse.

And yet, when one comes to think upon it calmly, the

situation of these South American citizens forms only a very pale figure for the state of ordinary mankind. This world itself, travelling blindly and swiftly in overcrowded space, among a million other worlds travelling blindly and swiftly in contrary directions, may very well come by a knock that would set it into explosion like a penny squib. And what, pathologically looked at, is the human body with all its organs, but a mere bagful of petards? The least of these is as dangerous to the whole economy as the ship's powder-magazine to the ship; and with every breath we breathe, and every meal we eat, we are putting one or more of them in peril. If we clung as devotedly as some philosophers pretend we do to the abstract idea of life, or were half as frightened as they make out we are, for the subversive accident that ends it all, the trumpets might sound by the hour and no one would follow them into battle—the blue-peter might fly at the truck, but who would climb into a sea-going ship? Think (if these philosophers were right) with what a preparation of spirit we should affront the daily peril of the dinner-table: a deadlier spot than any battle-field in history, where the far greater proportion of our ancestors have miserably left their bones! What woman would ever be lured into marriage, so much more dangerous than the wildest sea? And what would it be to grow old? For, after a certain distance, every step we take in life we find the ice growing thinner below our feet, and all around us and behind us we see our contemporaries going through. By the time a man gets well into the seventies, his continued existence is a mere miracle; and when he lays his old bones in bed for the night, there is an overwhelming probability that he will never see the day. Do the old men mind it, as a matter of fact?

Why, no. They were never merrier; they have their grog at night, and tell the raciest stories; they hear of the death of people about their own age, or even younger, not as if it was a grisly warning, but with a simple child-like pleasure at having outlived some one else; and when a draught might puff them out like a guttering candle, or a bit of a stumble shatter them like so much glass, their old hearts keep sound and unaffrighted, and they go on, bubbling with laughter, through years of man's age compared to which the valley at Balaklava was as safe and peaceful as a village cricket-green on Sunday. It may fairly be questioned (if we look to the peril only) whether it was a much more daring feat for Curtius to plunge into the gulf, than for any old gentleman of ninety to doff his clothes and clamber into bed.

Indeed, it is a memorable subject for consideration, with what unconcern and gaiety mankind pricks on along the Valley of the Shadow of Death. The whole way is one wilderness of snares, and the end of it, for those who fear the last pinch, is irrevocable ruin. And yet we go spinning through it all, like a party for the Derby. Perhaps the reader remembers one of the humorous devices of the deified Caligula: how he encouraged a vast concourse of holiday-makers on to his bridge over Baiæ bay; and when they were in the height of their enjoyment, turned loose the Prætorian guards among the company, and had them tossed into the sea. This is no bad miniature of the dealings of nature with the transitory race of man. Only, what a chequered picnic we have of it, even while it lasts! and into what great waters, not to be crossed by any swimmer, God's pale Prætorian throws us over in the end!

We live the time that a match flickers; we pop the

cork of a ginger-beer bottle, and the earthquake swallows us on the instant. Is it not odd, is it not incongruous, is it not, in the highest sense of human speech, incredible, that we should think so highly of the ginger-beer, and regard so little the devouring earthquake? The love of Life and the fear of Death are two famous phrases that grow harder to understand the more we think about them. It is a well-known fact that an immense proportion of boat accidents would never happen if people held the sheet in their hands instead of making it fast; and yet, unless it be some martinet of a professional mariner or some landsman with shattered nerves, every one of God's creatures makes it fast. A strange instance of man's unconcern and brazen boldness in the face of death!

We confound ourselves with metaphysical phrases, which we import into daily talk with noble inappropriateness. We have no idea of what death is, apart from its circumstances and some of its consequences to others; and although we have some experience of living, there is not a man on earth who has flown so high into abstraction as to have any practical guess at the meaning of the word *life*. All literature, from Job and Omar Khayam to Thomas Carlyle or Walt Whitman, is but an attempt to look upon the human state with such largeness of view as shall enable us to rise from the consideration of living to the Definition of Life. And our sages give us about the best satisfaction in their power when they say that it is a vapour, or a show, or made out of the same stuff with dreams. Philosophy, in its more rigid sense, has been at the same work for ages; and after a myriad bald heads have wagged over the problem, and piles of words have been heaped one upon another into dry and cloudy volumes without end, philosophy has the honour of laying before us, with modest pride, her contribution towards the subject: that life is a Permanent Possibility of Sensation. Truly a fine result! A man may very well love beef, or hunting, or a woman; but surely, surely, not a Permanent Possibility of Sensation! He may be afraid of a precipice, or a dentist, or a large enemy with a club, or even an undertaker's man; but not certainly of abstract death. We may trick with the word life in its dozen senses until we are weary of tricking; we may argue in terms of all the philosophies on earth, but one fact remains true throughout—that we do not love life, in the sense that we are greatly preoccupied about its conservation; that we do not, properly speaking, love life at all, but living. Into the views of the least careful there will enter some degree of providence; no man's eyes are fixed entirely on the passing hour; but although we have some anticipation of good health, good weather, wine, active employment, love, and self-approval, the sum of these anticipations does not amount to anything like a general view of life's possibilities and issues; nor are those who cherish them most vividly, at all the most scrupulous of their personal safety. To be deeply interested in the accidents of our existence, to enjoy keenly the mixed texture of human experience, rather leads a man to disregard precautions, and risk his neck against a straw. For surely the love of living is stronger in an Alpine climber roping over a peril, or a hunter riding merrily at a stiff fence, than in a creature who lives upon a diet and walks a measured distance in the interest of his constitution.

There is a great deal of very vile nonsense talked upon both sides of the matter: tearing divines reducing life to the dimensions of a mere funeral procession, so short as to be hardly decent; and melancholy unbelievers yearning for the tomb as if it were a world too far away. Both sides must feel a little ashamed of their performances now and again when they draw in their chairs to dinner. Indeed, a good meal and a bottle of wine is an answer to most standard works upon the question. When a man's heart warms to his viands, he forgets a great deal of sophistry, and soars into a rosy zone of contemplation. Death may be knocking at the door, like the Commander's statue; we have something else in hand, thank God, and let him knock. Passing bells are ringing all the world over. All the world over, and every hour, some one is parting company with all his aches and ecstasies. For us also the trap is laid. But we are so fond of life that we have no leisure to entertain the terror of death. It is a honeymoon with us all through, and none of the longest. Small blame to us if we give our whole hearts to this glowing bride of ours, to the appetites, to honour, to the hungry curiosity of the mind, to the pleasure of the eyes in nature, and the pride of our own nimble bodies.

We all of us appreciate the sensations; but as for caring about the Permanence of the Possibility, a man's head is generally very bald, and his senses very dull, before he comes to that. Whether we regard life as a lane leading to a dead wall—a mere bag's end, as the French say—or whether we think of it as a vestibule or gymnasium, where we wait our turn and prepare our faculties for some more noble destiny; whether we thunder in a pulpit, or pule in little atheistic poetry-books, about its vanity and brevity; whether we look justly for years of health and vigour, or are about to mount into a bath-chair, as a step towards the hearse; in each and all of these views and situations there is but one conclusion possible: that a man should stop his ears against paralysing terror, and run the race that is set before him with a single mind. No one surely could have recoiled with more heartache and terror from the thought of death than our respected lexicographer; and yet we know how little it affected his conduct, how wisely and boldly he walked, and in what a fresh and lively vein he spoke of life. Already an old man, he ventured on his Highland tour; and his heart, bound with triple brass, did not recoil before twenty-seven individual cups of tea. As courage and intelligence are the two qualities best worth a good man's cultivation, so it is the first part of intelligence to recognise our precarious estate in life, and the first part of courage to be not at all abashed before the fact. A frank and somewhat headlong carriage, not looking too anxiously before, not dallying in maudlin regret over the past, stamps the man who is well armoured for this world.

And not only well armoured for himself, but a good friend and a good citizen to boot. We do not go to cowards for tender dealing; there is nothing so cruel as panic; the man who has least fear for his own carcase, has most time to consider others. That eminent chemist who took his walks abroad in tin shoes, and subsisted wholly upon tepid milk, had all his work cut out for him in considerate dealings with his own digestion. So soon as prudence has begun to grow up in the brain, like a dismal fungus, it finds its first expression in a paralysis of generous acts. The victim begins to shrink spiritually; he develops a fancy for parlours with a regulated temperature, and takes his morality on the principle of tin shoes and tepid milk.

The care of one important body or soul becomes so engrossing, that all the noises of the outer world begin to come thin and faint into the parlour with the regulated temperature; and the tin shoes go equably forward over blood and rain. To be overwise is to ossify; and the scruple-monger ends by standing stockstill. Now the man who has his heart on his sleeve, and a good whirling weathercock of a brain, who reckons his life as a thing to be dashingly used and cheerfully hazarded, makes a very different acquaintance of the world, keeps all his pulses going true and fast, and gathers impetus as he runs, until, if he be running towards anything better than wildfire, he may shoot up and become a constellation in the end. Lord look after his health, Lord have a care of his soul, says he; and he has at the key of the position, and swashes through incongruity and peril towards his aim. Death is on all sides of him with pointed batteries, as he is on all sides of all of us; unfortunate surprises gird him round; mim-mouthed friends and relations hold up their hands in quite a little elegiacal synod about his path: and what cares he for all this? Being a true lover of living, a fellow with something pushing and spontaneous in his inside, he must, like any other soldier, in any other stirring, deadly warfare, push on at his best pace until he touch the goal. "A peerage or Westminster Abbey!" cried Nelson in his bright, boyish, heroic manner. These are great incentives; not for any of these, but for the plain satisfaction of living, of being about their business in some sort or other, do the brave, serviceable men of every nation tread down the nettle danger, and pass flyingly over all the stumbling-blocks of prudence. Think of the heroism of Johnson, think of that superb indifference to mortal limitation that set him upon his dictionary, and carried him through triumphantly until the end! Who, if he were wisely considerate of things at large, would ever embark upon any work much more considerable than a halfpenny postcard? Who would project a serial novel, after Thackeray and Dickens had each fallen in mid-course? Who would find heart enough to begin to live, if he dallied with the consideration of death?

And, after all, what sorry and pitiful quibbling all this is! To forego all the issues of living in a parlour with a regulated temperature—as if that were not to die a hundred times over, and for ten years at a stretch! As if it were not to die in one's own lifetime, and without even the sad immunities of death! As if it were not to die, and yet be the patient spectators of our own pitiable change! The Permanent Possibility is preserved, but the sensations carefully held at arm's length, as if one kept a photographic plate in a dark chamber. It is better to lose health like a spendthrift than to waste it like a miser. It is better to live and be done with it, than to die daily in the sick-room. By all means begin your folio; even if the doctor does not give you a year, even if he hesitates about a month, make one brave push and see what can be accomplished in a week. It is not only in finished undertakings that we ought to honour useful labour. A spirit goes out of the man who means execution, which outlives the most untimely ending. All who have meant good work with their whole hearts, have done good work, although they may die before they have the time to sign it. Every heart that has beat strong and cheerfully has left a hopeful impulse behind it in the world, and bettered the tradition of mankind. And even if death catch people, like an open pitfall, and in mid-career, laying out vast projects, and planning monstrous foundations, flushed with hope, and their mouths full of boastful language, they should be at once tripped up and silenced: is there not something brave and spirited in such a termination? and does not life go down with a better grace, foaming in full body over a precipice, than miserably straggling to an end in sandy deltas? When the Greeks made their fine saying that those whom the gods love die young, I cannot help believing they had this sort of death also in their eye. For surely, at whatever age it overtake the man, this is to die young. Death has not been suffered to take so much as an illusion from his heart. In the hot-fit of life, a-tiptoe on the highest point of being, he passes at a bound on to the other side. The noise of the mallet and chisel is scarcely quenched, the trumpets are hardly done blowing, when, trailing with him clouds of glory, this happy-starred, full-blooded spirit shoots into the spiritual land.

# EL DORADO

# EL DORADO

It seems as if a great deal were attainable in a world where there are so many marriages and decisive battles, and where we all, at certain hours of the day, and with great gusto and despatch, stow a portion of victuals finally and irretrievably into the bag which contains us. And it would seem also, on a hasty view, that the attainment of as much as possible was the one goal of man's contentious life. And yet, as regards the spirit, this is but a semblance. We live in an ascending scale when we live happily, one thing leading to another in an endless series. There is always a new horizon for onward-looking men, and although we dwell on a small planet, immersed in petty business and not enduring beyond a brief period of years, we are so constituted that our hopes are inaccessible, like stars, and the term of hoping is prolonged until the term of life. To be truly happy is a question of how we begin and not of how we end, of what we want and not of what we have. An aspiration is a joy for ever, a possession as solid as a landed estate, a fortune which we can never exhaust and which gives us year by year a revenue of pleasurable activity. To have many of these is to be spiritually rich. Life is only a very dull and ill-directed theatre unless we have some interests in the piece; and to those who have neither art nor science, the world is a mere arrangement of colours, or a rough footway where they may very well break their shins. It is in virtue of his own desires and curiosities that any man continues to exist with even patience, that he is charmed by the look of things and people, and that he wakens every morning with a renewed appetite for work and pleasure. Desire and curiosity are the two eyes through which he sees the world in the most enchanted colours: it is they that make women beautiful or fossils interesting: and the man may squander his estate and come to beggary, but if he keeps these two amulets he is still rich in the possibilities of pleasure. Suppose he could take one meal so compact and comprehensive that he should never hunger any more; suppose him, at a glance, to take in all the features of the world and allay the desire for knowledge; suppose him to do the like in any province of experience—would not that man be in a poor way for amusement ever after?

One who goes touring on foot with a single volume in his knapsack reads with circumspection, pausing often to reflect, and often laying the book down to contemplate the landscape or the prints in the inn parlour; for he fears to come to an end of his entertainment, and be left companionless on the last stages of his journey. A young fellow recently finished the works of Thomas Carlyle, winding up, if we remember aright, with the ten notebooks upon Frederick the Great. "What!" cried the young fellow, in consternation, "is there no more Carlyle? Am I left to the daily papers?" A more celebrated instance is that of Alexander, who wept bitterly because he had no more worlds to subdue. And when Gibbon had finished the *Decline and Fall*, he had only a few moments of joy; and it was with a "sober melancholy" that he parted from his labours.

Happily we all shoot at the moon with ineffectual arrows; our hopes are set on inaccessible El Dorado; we come to an end of nothing here below. Interests are only plucked up to sow themselves again, like mustard. You would think, when the child was born, there would be an end to trouble; and yet it is only the beginning of fresh anxieties; and when you have seen it through its teething and its education, and at last its marriage, alas! it is only to have new fears, new quivering sensibilities, with every day; and the health of your children's children grows as touching a concern as that of your own. Again, when you have married your wife, you would think you were got upon a hilltop, and might begin to go downward by an easy slope. But you have only ended courting to begin marriage. Falling in love and winning love are often difficult tasks to overbearing and rebellious spirits; but to keep in love is also a business of some importance, to which both man and wife must bring kindness and goodwill. The true love story commences at the altar, when there lies before the married pair a most beautiful contest of wisdom and generosity, and a life-long struggle towards an unattainable ideal. Unattainable? Ay, surely unattainable, from the very fact that they are two instead of one.

"Of making books there is no end," complained the Preacher; and did not perceive how highly he was praising letters as an occupation. There is no end, indeed, to making books or experiments, or to travel, or to gathering wealth. Problem gives rise to problem. We may study for ever, and we are never as learned as we would. We have never made a statue worthy of our dreams. And when we have discovered a continent, or crossed a chain of mountains, it is only to find another ocean or another plain upon the farther side. In the infinite universe there is room for our swiftest diligence and to spare. It is not like the works of Carlyle, which can be read to an end. Even in a corner of it, in a private park, or in the neighbourhood of a single hamlet, the weather and the seasons keep so deftly changing that although we walk there for a lifetime there will be always something new to startle and delight us.

There is only one wish realisable on the earth; only one thing that can be perfectly attained: Death. And from a variety of circumstances we have no one to tell us whether it be worth attaining.

A strange picture we make on our way to our Chimæras, ceaselessly marching, grudging ourselves the time for rest; indefatigable, adventurous pioneers. It is true that we shall never reach the goal; it is even more than probable that there is no such place; and if we lived for centuries and were endowed with the powers of a god, we should find ourselves not much nearer what we wanted at the end. O toiling hands of mortals! O unwearied feet, travelling ye know not whither. Soon, soon, it seems to you, you must come forth on some conspicuous hilltop, and but a little way farther, against the setting sun, descry the spires of El Dorado. Little do ye know your own blessedness; for to travel hopefully is a better thing than to arrive, and the true success is to labour.

# THE ENGLISH ADMIRALS

# THE ENGLISH ADMIRALS

"Whether it be wise in men to do such actions or no, I am sure it is so in States to honour them."—SIR WILLIAM TEMPLE.

THERE is one story of the wars of Rome which I have always very much envied for England. Germanicus was going down at the head of the legions into a dangerous river—on the opposite bank the woods were full of Germans—when there flew out seven great eagles which seemed to marshal the Romans on their way; they did not pause or waver, but disappeared into the forest where the enemy lay concealed. "Forward!" cried Germanicus, with a fine rhetorical inspiration, "Forward! and follow the Roman birds." It would be a very heavy spirit that did not give a leap at such a signal, and a very timorous one that continued to have any doubt of success. To appropriate the eagles as fellow-countrymen was to make imaginary allies of the forces of nature; the Roman Empire and its military fortunes, and along with these the prospects of those individual Roman legionaries now fording a river in Germany, looked altogether greater and more hopeful. It is a kind of illusion easy to produce. A particular shape of cloud, the appearance of a particular star, the holiday of some particular saint, anything in short to remind the combatants of patriotic legends or old successes, may be enough to change the issue of a pitched battle; for it gives to the one party a feeling that Right and the larger interests are with them.

If an Englishman wishes to have such a feeling, it must be about the sea. The lion is nothing to us; he has not been taken to the hearts of the people, and naturalised as an English emblem. We know right well that a lion would fall foul of us as grimly as he would of a Frenchman or a Moldavian Jew, and we do not carry him before us in the smoke of battle. But the sea is our approach and bulwark; it has been the scene of our greatest triumphs and dangers; and we are accustomed in lyrical strains to claim it as our own. The prostrating experiences of foreigners between Calais and Dover have always an agreeable side to English prepossessions. A man from Bedfordshire, who does not know one end of the ship from the other until she begins to move, swaggers among such persons with a sense of hereditary nautical experience. To suppose yourself endowed with natural parts for the sea because you are the countryman of Blake and mighty Nelson, is perhaps just as unwarrantable as to imagine Scotch extraction a sufficient guarantee that you will look well in a kilt. But the feeling is there, and seated beyond the reach of argument. We should consider ourselves unworthy of our descent if we did not share the arrogance of our progenitors, and please ourselves with the pretension that the sea is English. Even where it is looked upon by the guns and battlements of another nation we regard it as a kind of English cemetery, where the bones of our seafaring fathers take their rest until the last trumpet; for I suppose no other nation has lost as many ships, or sent as many brave fellows to the bottom.

There is nowhere such a background for heroism as

the noble, terrifying, and picturesque conditions of some of our sea-fights. Hawke's battle in the tempest, and Aboukir at the moment when the French Admiral blew up, reach the limit of what is imposing to the imagination. And our naval annals owe some of their interest to the fantastic and beautiful appearance of old warships and the romance that invests the sea and everything sea-going in the eyes of English lads on a half-holiday at the coast. Nay, and what we know of the misery between decks enhances the bravery of what was done by giving it something for contrast. We like to know that these bold and honest fellows contrived to live, and to keep bold and honest, among absurd and vile surroundings. No reader can forget the description of the *Thunder* in *Roderick Random:* the disorderly tyranny; the cruelty and dirt of officers and men; deck after deck, each with some new object of offence; the hospital, where the hammocks were huddled together with but fourteen inches space for each; the cockpit, far under water, where, "in an intolerable stench," the spectacled steward kept the accounts of the different messes; and the canvas enclosure, six feet square, in which Morgan made flip and salmagundi, smoked his pipe, sang his Welsh songs, and swore his queer Welsh imprecations. There are portions of this business on board the *Thunder* over which the reader passes lightly and hurriedly, like a traveller in a malarious country. It is easy enough to understand the opinion of Dr. Johnson: "Why, sir," he said, "no man will be a sailor who has contrivance enough to get himself into a jail." You would fancy any one's spirit would die out under such an accumulation of darkness, noisomeness, and injustice, above all when he had not come there of his own free will, but under the cutlasses and bludgeons of the press-gang. But perhaps a watch on deck in the sharp sea air put a man on his mettle again; a battle must have been a capital relief; and prize-money, bloodily earned and grossly squandered, opened the doors of the prison for a twinkling. Somehow or other, at least, this worst of possible lives could not overlie the spirit and gaiety of our sailors; they did their duty as though they had some interest in the fortune of that country which so cruelly oppressed them, they served their guns merrily when it came to fighting, and they had the readiest ear for a bold, honourable sentiment, of any class of men the world ever produced.

Most men of high destinies have high-sounding names. Pym and Habakkuk may do pretty well, but they must not think to cope with the Cromwells and Isaiahs. And you could not find a better case in point than that of the English Admirals. Drake and Rooke and Hawke are picked names for men of execution. Frobisher, Rodney, Boscawen, Foul-Weather Jack Byron are all good to catch the eye in a page of a naval history. Cloudesley Shovel is a mouthful of quaint and sounding syllables. Benbow has a bull-dog quality that suits the man's character, and it takes us back to those English archers who were his true comrades for plainness, tenacity, and pluck. Raleigh is spirited and martial, and signifies an act of bold conduct in the field. It is impossible to judge of Blake or Nelson, no names current among men being worthy of such heroes. But still it is odd enough, and very appropriate in this connection, that the latter was greatly taken with his Sicilian title. "The signification, perhaps, pleased him," says Southey; "Duke of Thunder was what in Dahomey would have been called a *strong name*; it was to a sailor's taste, and certainly to no man could it be more applicable." Admiral in itself is one of the most satisfactory of distinctions; it has a noble sound and a very proud history; and Columbus thought so highly of it, that he enjoined his heirs to sign themselves by that title as long as the house should last.

But it is the spirit of the men, and not their names, that I wish to speak about in this paper. That spirit is truly English; they, and not Tennyson's cotton-spinners or Mr. D'Arcy Thompson's Abstract Bagman, are the true and typical Englishmen. There may be more *head* of bagmen in the country, but human beings are reckoned by number only in political constitutions. And the Admirals are typical in the full force of the word. They are splendid examples of virtue, indeed, but of a virtue in which most Englishmen can claim a moderate share; and what we admire in their lives is a sort of apotheosis of ourselves. Almost everybody in our land, except humanitarians and a few persons whose youth has been depressed by exceptionally æsthetic surroundings, can understand and sympathise with an Admiral or a prize-fighter. I do not wish to bracket Benbow and Tom Cribb; but, depend upon it, they are practically bracketed for admiration in the minds of many frequenters of ale-houses. If you told them about Germanicus and the eagles, or Regulus going back to Carthage, they would very likely fall asleep; but tell them about Harry Pearce and Jem Belcher, or about Nelson and the Nile, and they put down their pipes to listen. I have by me a copy of *Boxiana*, on the fly-leaves of which a youthful member of the fancy kept a chronicle of remarkable events and an obituary of great men. Here we find piously chronicled the demise of jockeys, watermen, and pugilists—Johnny Moore, of the Liverpool Prize Ring;

Tom Spring, aged fifty-six; "Pierce Egan, senior, writer of *Boxiana* and other sporting works"—and among all these, the Duke of Wellington! If Benbow had lived in the time of this annalist, do you suppose his name would not have been added to the glorious roll? In short, we do not all feel warmly towards Wesley or Laud, we cannot all take pleasure in *Paradise Lost;* but there are certain common sentiments and touches of nature by which the whole nation is made to feel kinship. A little while ago everybody, from Hazlitt and John Wilson down to the imbecile creature who scribbled his register on the fly-leaves of *Boxiana*, felt a more or less shamefaced satisfaction in the exploits of prize-fighters. And the exploits of the Admirals are popular to the same degree, and tell in all ranks of society. Their sayings and doings stir English blood like the sound of a trumpet; and if the Indian Empire, the trade of London, and all the outward and visible ensigns of our greatness should pass away, we should still leave behind us a durable monument of what we were in these sayings and doings of the English Admirals.

Duncan, lying off the Texel with his own flagship, the *Venerable*, and only one other vessel, heard that the whole Dutch fleet was putting to sea. He told Captain Hotham to anchor alongside of him in the narrowest part of the channel, and fight his vessel till she sank. "I have taken the depth of the water," added he, "and when the *Venerable* goes down, my flag will still fly." And you observe this is no naked Viking in a pre-historic period; but a Scotch member of Parliament, with a smattering of the classics, a telescope, a cocked hat of great size, and flannel underclothing. In the same spirit, Nelson went into Aboukir with six colours flying; so that even if five were shot away, it should not be imagined he had struck. He too must needs wear his four stars outside his Admiral's frock, to be a butt for sharp-shooters. "In honour I gained them," he said to objectors, adding with sublime illogicality, "in honour I will die with them." Captain Douglas of the *Royal Oak*, when the Dutch fired his vessel in the Thames, sent his men ashore, but was burned along with her himself rather than desert his post without orders. Just then, perhaps the Merry Monarch was chasing a moth round the supper-table with the ladies of his court. When Raleigh sailed into Cadiz, and all the forts and ships opened fire on him at once, he scorned to shoot a gun, and made answer with a flourish of insulting trumpets. I like this bravado better than the wisest dispositions to ensure victory; it comes from the heart and goes to it. God has made nobler heroes, but he never made a finer gentleman than Walter Raleigh. And as our Admirals were full of heroic superstitions, and had a strutting and vainglorious style of fight, so they discovered a startling eagerness for battle, and courted war like a mistress. When the news came to Essex before Cadiz that the attack had been decided, he threw his hat into the sea. It is in this way that a schoolboy hears of a half-holiday; but this was a bearded man of great possessions who had just been allowed to risk his life. Benbow could not lie still in his bunk after he had lost his leg; he must be on deck in a basket to direct and animate the fight. I said they loved war like a mistress; yet I think there are not many mistresses we should continue to woo under similar circumstances. Trowbridge went ashore with the *Culloden*, and was able to take no part in the battle of the Nile.

"The merits of that ship and her gallant captain," wrote Nelson to the Admiralty, "are too well known to benefit by anything I could say. Her misfortune was great in getting aground, *while her more fortunate companions were in the full tide of happiness*." This is a notable expression, and depicts the whole great-hearted, big-spoken stock of the English Admirals to a hair. It was to be "in the full tide of happiness" for Nelson to destroy five thousand five hundred and twenty-five of his fellow-creatures, and have his own scalp torn open by a piece of langridge shot. Hear him again at Copenhagen: "A shot through the mainmast knocked the splinters about; and he observed to one of his officers with a smile, 'It is warm work, and this may be the last to any of us at any moment;' and then, stopping short at the gangway, added, with emotion, '*But, mark you—I would not be elsewhere for thousands*.'"

I must tell one more story, which has lately been made familiar to us all, and that in one of the noblest ballads in the English language. I had written my tame prose abstract, I shall beg the reader to believe, when I had no notion that the sacred bard designed an immortality for Greenville. Sir Richard Greenville was Vice-Admiral to Lord Thomas Howard, and lay off the Azores with the English squadron in 1591. He was a noted tyrant to his crew: a dark, bullying fellow apparently; and it is related of him that he would chew and swallow wine-glasses, by way of convivial levity, till the blood ran out of his mouth. When the Spanish fleet of fifty sail came within sight of the English, his ship, the *Revenge*, was the last to weigh anchor, and was so far circumvented by the Spaniards, that there were but two courses open—either to turn her back upon the enemy or sail through one of his squadrons. The first alternative Greenville dismissed as dishonourable to himself, his country, and her Majesty's ship. Accordingly, he chose the latter, and steered into the Spanish armament. Several vessels he forced to luff and fall under his lee; until, about three o'clock of the afternoon, a great ship of three decks of ordnance took the wind out of his sails, and immediately boarded. Thenceforward, and all night long, the *Revenge* held her own single-handed against the Spaniards. As one ship was beaten off, another took its place. She endured, according to Raleigh's computation, "eight hundred shot of great artillery, besides many assaults and entries." By morning the powder was spent, the pikes all broken, not a stick was standing, "nothing left overhead either for flight or defence;" six feet of water in the hold; almost all the men hurt; and Greenville himself in a dying condition. To bring them to this pass, a fleet of fifty sail had been mauling them for fifteen hours, the *Admiral of the Hulks* and the *Ascension* of Seville had both gone down alongside, and two other vessels had taken refuge on shore in a sinking state. In Hawke's words, they had "taken a great deal of drubbing." The captain and crew thought they had done about enough; but Greenville was not of this opinion; he gave orders to the master-gunner, whom he knew to be a fellow after his own stamp, to scuttle the *Revenge* where she lay. The others, who were not mortally wounded like the Admiral, interfered with some decision, locked the master-gunner in his cabin, after having deprived him of his sword, for he manifested an intention to kill himself if he were not to sink the ship; and sent to the Spaniards to demand terms. These were granted. The second or third day after, Greenville died of his wounds aboard the Spanish flagship, leaving his contempt upon the "traitors and dogs" who had not chosen to do as he did, and engage fifty vessels, well found and fully manned, with six inferior craft ravaged by sickness and short of stores. He at least, he said, had done his duty as he was bound to do, and looked for everlasting fame.

Some one said to me the other day that they considered this story to be of a pestilent example. I am not inclined to imagine we shall ever be put into any practical difficulty from a superfluity of Greenvilles. And besides, I demur to the opinion. The worth of such actions is not a thing to be decided in a quaver of sensibility or a flush of righteous common-sense. The man who wished to make the ballads of his country, coveted a small matter compared to what Richard Greenville accomplished. I wonder how many people have been inspired by this mad story, and how many battles have been actually won for England in the spirit thus engendered. It is only with a measure of habitual foolhardiness that you can be sure, in the common run of men, of courage on a reasonable occasion. An army or a fleet, if it is not led by quixotic fancies, will not be led far by terror of the Provost-Marshal. Even German warfare, in addition to maps and telegraphs, is not above employing the *Wacht am Rhein*. Nor is it only in the profession of arms that such stories may do good to a man. In this desperate and gleeful fighting, whether it is Greenville or Benbow, Hawke or Nelson, who flies his colours in the ship, we see men brought to the test and giving proof of what we call heroic feeling. Prosperous humanitarians tell me, in my club smoking-room, that they are a prey to prodigious heroic feelings, and that it costs them more nobility of soul to do nothing in particular, than would carry on all the wars, by sea or land, of bellicose humanity. It may very well be so, and yet not touch the point in question. For what I desire is to see some of this nobility brought face to face with me in an inspiriting achievement. A man may talk smoothly over a cigar in my club smoking-room from now to the Day of Judgment, without adding anything to mankind's treasury of illustrious and encouraging examples. It is not over the virtues of a curate-and-tea-party novel, that people are abashed into high resolutions. It may be because their hearts are crass, but to stir them properly they must have men entering into glory with some pomp and circumstance. And that is why these stories of our sea-captains, printed, so to speak, in capitals, and full of bracing moral influence, are more valuable to England than any material benefit in all the books of political economy between Westminster and Birmingham. Greenville chewing wine-glasses at table makes no very pleasant figure, any more than a thousand other artists when they are viewed in the body, or met in private life; but his work of art, his finished tragedy, is an eloquent performance; and I contend it ought not only to enliven men of the sword as they go into battle, but send back merchant-clerks with more heart and spirit to their book-keeping by double entry.

There is another question which seems bound up in this; and that is Temple's problem: whether it was wise of Douglas to burn with the *Royal Oak?* and by implication, what it was that made him do so? Many will tell you it was the desire of fame.

"To what do Cæsar and Alexander owe the infinite grandeur of their renown, but to fortune? How many men has she extinguished in the beginning of their progress, of whom we have no knowledge; who brought as much courage to the work as they, if their adverse hap had not cut them off in the first sally of their arms? Amongst so many and so great dangers, I do not remember to have anywhere read that Cæsar was ever wounded; a thousand have fallen in less dangers than the least of these he went through. A great many brave actions must be expected to be performed without witness, for one that comes to some notice. A man is not always at the top of a breach, or at the head of an army in the sight of his general, as upon a platform. He is often surprised between the hedge and the ditch; he must run the hazard of his life against a hen-roost; he must dislodge four rascally musketeers out of a barn; he must prick out single from his party, as necessity arises, and meet adventures alone."

Thus far Montaigne, in a characteristic essay on *Glory*. Where death is certain, as in the cases of Douglas or Greenville, it seems all one from a personal point of view. The man who lost his life against a hen-roost is in the same pickle with him who lost his life against a fortified place of the first order. Whether he has missed a peerage or only the corporal's stripes, it is all one if he has missed them and is quietly in the grave. It was by a hazard that we learned the conduct of the four marines of the *Wager*. There was no room for these brave fellows in the boat, and they were left behind upon the island to a certain death. They were soldiers, they said, and knew well enough it was their business to die; and as their comrades pulled away they stood upon the beach, gave three cheers, and cried "God bless the king!" Now, one or two of those who were in the boat escaped, against all likelihood, to tell the story. That was a great thing for us; but surely it cannot, by any possible twisting of human speech, be construed into anything great for the marines. You may suppose, if you like, that they died hoping their behaviour would not be forgotten; or you may suppose they thought nothing on the subject, which is much more likely. What can be the signification of the word "fame" to a private of marines, who cannot read and knows nothing of past history beyond the reminiscences of his grandmother? But whichever supposition you make, the fact is unchanged. They died while the question still hung in the balance; and I suppose their bones were already white, before the winds and the waves and the humour of Indian chiefs and Spanish governors had decided whether they were to be unknown and useless martyrs or honoured heroes. Indeed, I believe this is the lesson: if it is for fame that men do brave actions, they are only silly fellows after all.

It is at best but a pettifogging, pickthank business to decompose actions into little personal motives, and explain heroism away. The Abstract Bagman will grow like an Admiral at heart, not by ungrateful carping, but in a heat of admiration. But there is another theory of the personal motive in these fine sayings and doings, which I believe to be true and wholesome. People usually do things, and suffer martyrdoms, because they have an inclination that way. The best artist is not the man who fixes his eye on posterity, but the one who loves the practice of his art. And instead of having a taste for being successful merchants and retiring at thirty, some people have a taste for high and what we call heroic forms of excitement. If the Admirals courted war like a mistress; if, as the drum beat to quarters, the sailors came gaily out of the forecastle,—it is because a fight is a period of multiplied and intense experiences, and, by Nelson's computation, worth "thousands" to any one who has a heart under his jacket. If the marines of the *Wager* gave three cheers and cried "God bless the king," it was because they liked to do things nobly for their own satisfaction. They were giving their lives, there was no help for that; and they made it a point of self-respect to give them handsomely. And there were never four happier marines in God's world than these four at that moment. If it was worth thousands to be at the Baltic, I wish a Benthamite arithmetician would calculate how much it was worth to be one of these four marines; or how much their story is worth to each of us who read it. And mark you, undemonstrative men would have spoiled the situation. The finest action is the better for a piece of purple. If the soldiers of the *Birkenhead* had not gone down in line, or these marines of the *Wager* had walked away simply into the island, like plenty of other brave fellows in the like circumstances, my Benthamite arithmetician would assign a far lower value to the two stories. We have to desire a grand air in our heroes; and such a knowledge of the human stage as shall make them put the dots on their own i's, and leave us in no suspense as to when they mean to be heroic. And hence, we should congratulate ourselves upon the fact that our Admirals were not only great-hearted but big-spoken.

The heroes themselves say, as often as not, that fame is their object; but I do not think that is much to the purpose. People generally say what they have been taught to say; that was the catchword they were given in youth to express the aims of their way of life; and men who are gaining great battles are not likely to take much trouble in reviewing their sentiments and the words in which they were told to express them. Almost every person, if you will believe himself, holds a quite different theory of life from the one on which he is patently acting. And the fact is, fame may be a forethought and an afterthought, but it is too abstract an idea to move people greatly in moments of swift and momentous decision. It is from something more immediate, some determination of blood to the head, some trick of the fancy, that the breach is stormed or the bold word spoken. I am sure a fellow shooting an ugly weir in a canoe has exactly as much thought about fame as most commanders going into battle; and yet the action, fall out how it will, is not one of those the muse delights to celebrate. Indeed it is difficult to see why the fellow does a thing so nameless and yet so formidable to look at, unless on the theory that he likes it. I suspect that is why; and I suspect it is at least ten per cent. of why Lord Beaconsfield and Mr. Gladstone have debated so much in the House of Commons, and why Burnaby rode to Khiva the other day, and why the Admirals courted war like a mistress.

# SOME PORTRAITS BY RAEBURN

# SOME PORTRAITS BY RAEBURN

THROUGH the initiative of a prominent citizen, Edinburgh has been in possession, for some autumn weeks, of a gallery of paintings of singular merit and interest. They were exposed in the apartments of the Scotch Academy; and filled those who are accustomed to visit the annual spring exhibition with astonishment and a sense of incongruity. Instead of the too common purple sunsets, and pea-green fields, and distances executed in putty and hog's lard, he beheld, looking down upon him from the walls of room after room, a whole army of wise, grave, humorous, capable, or beautiful countenances, painted simply and strongly by a man of genuine instinct. It was a complete act of the Human Drawing-Room Comedy. Lords and ladies, soldiers and doctors, hanging judges and heretical divines, a whole generation of good society was resuscitated; and the Scotchman of to-day walked about among the Scotchmen of two generations ago. The moment was well chosen, neither too late nor too early. The people who sat for these pictures are not yet ancestors, they are still relations. They are not yet altogether a part of the dusty past, but occupy a middle distance within cry of our affections. The little child who looks wonderingly on his grandfather's watch in the picture is now the veteran Sheriff *emeritus* of Perth. And I hear a story of a lady who returned the other day to

Edinburgh, after an absence of sixty years: "I could see none of my old friends," she said, "until I went into the Raeburn Gallery, and found them all there."

It would be difficult to say whether the collection was more interesting on the score of unity or diversity. Where the portraits were all of the same period, almost all of the same race and all from the same brush, there could not fail to be many points of similarity. And yet the similarity of the handling seems to throw into more vigorous relief those personal distinctions which Raeburn was so quick to seize. He was a born painter of portraits. He looked people shrewdly between the eyes, surprised their manners in their face, and had possessed himself of what was essential in their character before they had been many minutes in his studio. What he was so swift to perceive, he conveyed to the canvas almost in the moment of conception. He had never any difficulty, he said, about either hands or faces. About draperies or light or composition, he might see room for hesitation or afterthought. But a face or a hand was something plain and legible. There were no two ways about it, any more than about the person's name. And so each of his portraits is not only (in Doctor Johnson's phrase, aptly quoted on the catalogue) "a piece of history," but a piece of biography into the bargain. It is devoutly to be wished that all biography were equally amusing, and carried its own credentials equally upon its face. These portraits are racier than many anecdotes, and more complete than many a volume of sententious memoirs. You can see whether you get a stronger and clearer idea of Robertson the historian from Raeburn's palette or Dugald Stewart's woolly and evasive periods. And then the portraits are both signed and countersigned. For you have, first, the authority of the artist, whom you recognise as no mean critic of the looks and manners of men; and next you have the tacit acquiescence of the subject, who sits looking out upon you with inimitable innocence, and apparently under the impression that he is in a room by himself. For Raeburn could plunge at once through all the constraint and embarrassment of the sitter, and present the face, clear, open, and intelligent as at the most disengaged moments. This is best seen in portraits where the sitter is represented in some appropriate action: Neil Gow with his fiddle, Doctor Spens shooting an arrow, or Lord Bannatyne hearing a cause. Above all, from this point of view, the portrait of Lieutenant-Colonel Lyon is notable. A strange enough young man, pink, fat about the lower part of the face, with a lean forehead, a narrow nose and a fine nostril, sits with a drawing-board upon his knees. He has just paused to render himself account of some difficulty, to disentangle some complication of line or compare neighbouring values. And there, without any perceptible wrinkling, you have rendered for you exactly the fixed look in the eyes, and the unconscious compression of the mouth, that befit and signify an effort of the kind. The whole pose, the whole expression, is absolutely direct and simple. You are ready to take your oath to it that Colonel Lyon had no idea he was sitting for his picture, and thought of nothing in the world besides his own occupation of the moment.

Although the collection did not embrace, I understand, nearly the whole of Raeburn's works, it was too large not to contain some that were indifferent, whether as works of art or as portraits. Certainly the standard was remarkably high, and was wonderfully maintained, but there were one or two pictures that might have been almost as well away—one or two that seemed wanting in salt, and some that you can only hope were not successful likenesses. Neither of the portraits of Sir Walter Scott, for instance, were very agreeable to look upon. You do not care to think that Scott looked quite so rustic and puffy. And where is that peaked forehead which, according to all written accounts and many portraits, was the distinguishing characteristic of his face? Again, in spite of his own satisfaction and in spite of Dr. John Brown, I cannot consider that Raeburn was very happy in hands. Without doubt, he could paint one if he had taken the trouble to study it; but it was by no means always that he gave himself the trouble. Looking round one of these rooms hung about with his portraits, you were struck with the array of expressive faces, as compared with what you may have seen in looking round a room full of living people. But it was not so with the hands. The portraits differed from each other in face perhaps ten times as much as they differed by the hand; whereas with living people the two go pretty much together; and where one is remarkable, the other will almost certainly not be commonplace.

One interesting portrait was that of Duncan of Camperdown. He stands in uniform beside a table, his feet slightly straddled with the balance of an old sailor, his hand poised upon a chart by the finger-tips. The mouth is pursed, the nostril spread and drawn up, the eyebrows very highly arched. The cheeks lie along the jaw in folds of iron, and have the redness that comes from much exposure to salt-sea winds. From the whole figure, attitude and countenance, there breathes something precise and decisive, something alert, wiry, and strong. You can understand, from the look of him, that sense, not so much of humour, as of what is grimmest and driest in pleasantry, which inspired his address before the fight at Camperdown. He had just overtaken the Dutch fleet under Admiral de Winter. "Gentlemen," says he, "you see a severe winter approaching; I have only to advise you to keep up a good fire." Somewhat of this same spirit of adamantine drollery must have supported him in the days of the mutiny at the Nore, when he lay off the Texel with his own flagship, the *Venerable*, and only one other vessel, and kept up active signals, as though he had a powerful fleet in the offing, to intimidate the Dutch.

Another portrait which irresistibly attracted the eye was the half-length of Robert M'Queen, of Braxfield, Lord Justice-Clerk. If I know gusto in painting when I see it, this canvas was painted with rare enjoyment. The tart, rosy, humorous look of the man, his nose like a cudgel, his face resting squarely on the jowl, has been caught and perpetuated with something that looks like brotherly love. A peculiarly subtle expression haunts the lower part, sensual and incredulous, like that of a man tasting good Bordeaux with half a fancy it has been somewhat too long uncorked. From under the pendulous eyelids of old age the eyes look out with a half-youthful, half-frosty twinkle. Hands, with no pretence to distinction, are folded on the judge's stomach. So sympathetically is the character conceived by the portrait-painter, that it is hardly possible to avoid some movement of sympathy on the part of the spectator. And sympathy is a thing to be encouraged, apart from humane considerations, because it supplies us with the materials for wisdom. It is probably more instructive to entertain a sneaking kindness for any unpopular person, and, among the rest, for Lord Braxfield, than to give way to perfect raptures of moral indignation against his abstract vices. He was the last judge on the Scotch bench to employ the pure Scotch idiom. His opinions, thus given in Doric, and conceived in a lively, rugged, conversational style, were full of point and authority. Out of the bar, or off the bench, he was a convivial man, a lover of wine, and one who "shone peculiarly" at tavern meetings. He has left behind him an unrivalled reputation for rough and cruel speech; and to this day his name smacks of the gallows. It was he who presided at the trials of Muir and Skirving in 1793 and 1794; and his appearance on these occasions was scarcely cut to the pattern of to day. His summing up on Muir began thus—the reader must supply for himself "the growling, blacksmith's voice" and the broad Scotch accent: "Now this is the question for consideration—Is the panel guilty of sedition, or is he not? Now, before this can be answered, two things must be attended to that require no proof: *First*, that the British constitution is the best that ever was since the creation of the world, and it is not possible to make it better." It's a pretty fair start, is it not, for a political trial? A little later, he has occasion to refer to the relations of Muir with "those wretches," the French. "I never liked the French all my days," said his lordship, "but now I hate them." And yet a little further on: "A government in any country should be like a corporation; and in this country it is made up of the landed interest, which alone has a right to be represented. As for the rabble who have nothing but personal property, what hold has the nation of them? They may pack up their property on their backs, and leave the country in the twinkling of an eye." After having made profession of sentiments so cynically anti-popular as these, when the trials were at an end, which was generally about midnight, Braxfield would walk home to his house in George Square with no better escort than an easy conscience. I think I see him getting his cloak about his shoulders, and, with perhaps a lantern in one hand, steering his way along the streets in the mirk January night. It might have been that very day that Skirving had defied him in these words: "It is altogether unavailing for your lordship to menace me; for I have long learned to fear not the face of man;" and I can fancy, as Braxfield reflected on the number of what he called *Grumbletonians* in Edinburgh, and of how many of them must bear special malice against so upright and inflexible a judge, nay, and might at that very moment be lurking in the mouth of a dark close with hostile intent—I can fancy that he indulged in a sour smile, as he reflected that he also was not especially afraid of men's faces or men's fists, and had hitherto found no occasion to embody this insensibility in heroic words. For if he was an inhumane old gentleman (and I am afraid it is a fact that he was inhumane), he was also perfectly intrepid. You may look into the queer face of that portrait for as long as you will, but you will not see any hole or corner for timidity to enter in.

Indeed, there would be no end to this paper if I were even to name half of the portraits that were remarkable for their execution, or interesting by association. There was one picture of Mr. Wardrop, of Torbane Hill, which you might palm off upon most laymen as a Rembrandt; and close by, you saw the white head of John Clerk, of Eldin, that country gentleman who, playing with pieces of cork on his own dining-table, invented modern naval warfare. There was that portrait of Neil Gow, to sit for which the old fiddler walked daily through the streets of Edinburgh arm in arm with the Duke of Athole. There was good Harry Erskine, with his satirical nose and upper lip, and his mouth just open for a witticism to pop out; Hutton the geologist, in quakerish raiment, and looking altogether trim and narrow, and as if he cared more about fossils than young ladies; full-blown John Robieson, in hyperbolical red dressing-gown, and, every inch of him, a fine old man of the world; Constable the publisher, upright beside a table, and bearing a corporation with commercial dignity; Lord Bannatyne hearing a cause, if ever anybody heard a cause since the world began; Lord Newton just awakened from clandestine slumber on the bench; and the second President Dundas, with every feature so fat that he reminds you, in his wig, of some droll old court officer in an illustrated nursery story-book, and yet all these fat features instinct with meaning, the fat lips curved and compressed, the nose combining somehow the dignity of a beak with the good nature of a bottle, and the very double chin with an air of intelligence and insight. And all these portraits are so pat and telling, and look at you so spiritedly from the walls, that, compared with the sort of living people one sees about the streets, they are as bright new sovereigns to fishy and obliterated sixpences. Some disparaging thoughts upon our own generation could hardly fail to present themselves; but it is perhaps only the *sacer vates* who is wanting; and we also, painted by such a man as Carolus Duran, may look in holiday immortality upon our children and grandchildren.

Raeburn's young women, to be frank, are by no means

of the same order of merit. No one, of course, could be insensible to the presence of Miss Janet Suttie or Mrs. Campbell of Possil. When things are as pretty as that, criticism is out of season. But, on the whole, it is only with women of a certain age that he can be said to have succeeded in at all the same sense as we say he succeeded with men. The younger women do not seem to be made of good flesh and blood. They are not painted in rich and unctuous touches. They are dry and diaphanous. And although young ladies in Great Britain are all that can be desired of them, I would fain hope they are not quite so much of that as Raeburn would have us believe. In all these pretty faces, you miss character, you miss fire, you miss that spice of the devil which is worth all the prettiness in the world; and what is worst of all, you miss sex. His young ladies are not womanly to nearly the same degree as his men are masculine; they are so in a negative sense; in short, they are the typical young ladies of the male novelist.

To say truth, either Raeburn was timid with young and pretty sitters; or he had stupefied himself with sentimentalities; or else (and here is about the truth of it) Raeburn and the rest of us labour under an obstinate blindness in one direction, and know very little more about women after all these centuries than Adam when he first saw Eve. This is all the more likely, because we are by no means so unintelligent in the matter of old women. There are some capital old women, it seems to me, in books written by men. And Raeburn has some, such as Mrs. Colin Campbell, of Park, or the anonymous "Old lady with a large cap," which are done in the same frank, perspicacious spirit as the very best of his men. He could look into their eyes without trouble; and he was not withheld, by any bashful sentimentalism, from recognising what he saw there and unsparingly putting it down upon the canvas. But where people cannot meet without some confusion and a good deal of involuntary humbug, and are occupied, for as long as they are together, with a very different vein of thought, there cannot be much room for intelligent study nor much result in the shape of genuine comprehension. Even women, who understand men so well for practical purposes, do not know them well enough for the purposes of art. Take even the very best of their male creations, take Tito Melema, for instance, and you will find he has an equivocal air, and every now and again remembers he has a comb at the back of his head. Of course, no woman will believe this, and many men will be so very polite as to humour their incredulity.

# CHILD'S PLAY

# CHILD'S PLAY

The regret we have for our childhood is not wholly justifiable: so much a man may lay down without fear of public ribaldry; for although we shake our heads over the change, we are not unconscious of the manifold advantages of our new state. What we lose in generous impulse, we more than gain in the habit of generously watching others; and the capacity to enjoy Shakespeare may balance a lost aptitude for playing at soldiers. Terror is gone out of our lives, moreover; we no longer see the devil in the bed-curtains nor lie awake to listen to the wind. We go to school no more; and if we have only exchanged one drudgery for another (which is by no means sure), we are set free for ever from the daily fear of chastisement. And yet a great change has overtaken us; and although we do not enjoy ourselves less, at least we take our pleasure differently. We need pickles nowadays to make Wednesday's cold mutton please our Friday's appetite; and I can remember the time when to call it red venison, and tell myself a hunter's story, would have made it more palatable than the best of sauces. To the grown person, cold mutton is cold mutton all the world over; not all the mythology ever invented by man will make it better or worse to him; the broad fact, the clamant reality, of the mutton carries away before it such seductive figments. But for the child it is still possible to weave an enchantment over eatables; and if he has but read of a dish in a story-book, it will be heavenly manna to him for a week.

If a grown man does not like eating and drinking and exercise, if he is not something positive in his tastes, it means he has a feeble body and should have some medicine; but children may be pure spirits, if they will, and take their enjoyment in a world of moonshine. Sensation does not count for so much in our first years as afterwards; something of the swaddling numbness of infancy clings about us; we see and touch and hear through a sort of golden mist. Children, for instance, are able enough to see, but they have no great faculty for looking; they do not use their eyes for the pleasure of using them, but for by-ends of their own; and the things I call to mind seeing most vividly, were not beautiful in themselves, but merely interesting or enviable to me as I thought they might be turned to practical account in play. Nor is the sense of touch so clean and poignant in children as it is in a man. If you will turn over your old memories, I think the sensations of this sort you remember will be somewhat vague, and come to not much more than a blunt, general sense of heat on summer days, or a blunt, general sense of well-being in bed. And here, of course, you will understand pleasurable sensations; for overmastering pain—the most deadly and tragical element in life, and the true commander of man's soul and body—alas! pain has its own way with all of us; it breaks in, a rude visitant, upon the fairy garden where the child wanders in a dream, no less surely than it rules upon the field of battle, or sends the immortal war-god whimpering to his father; and innocence, no more than philosophy, can protect us from this sting. As for taste, when we bear in mind the excesses of unmitigated sugar which delight a youthful palate, "it is surely no very cynical asperity" to think taste a character of the maturer growth. Smell and hearing are perhaps more developed; I remember many scents, many voices, and a great deal of spring singing in the woods. But hearing is capable of vast improvement as a means of pleasure; and there is all the world between gaping wonderment at the jargon of birds, and the emotion with which a man listens to articulate music.

At the same time, and step by step with this increase in the definition and intensity of what we feel which accompanies our growing age, another change takes place in the sphere of intellect, by which all things are transformed and seen through theories and associations as through coloured windows. We make to ourselves day by day, out of history, and gossip, and economical speculations, and God knows what, a medium in which we walk and through which we look abroad. We study shop windows with other eyes than in our childhood, never to wonder, not always to admire, but to make and modify our little incongruous theories about life. It is no longer the uniform of a soldier that arrests our attention; but perhaps the flowing carriage of a woman, or perhaps a countenance that has been vividly stamped with passion and carries an adventurous story written in its lines. The pleasure of surprise is passed away; sugar-loaves and water-carts seem mighty tame to encounter; and we walk the streets to make romances and to sociologise. Nor must we deny that a good many of us walk them solely for the purposes of transit or in the interest of a livelier digestion. These, indeed, may look back with mingled thoughts upon their childhood, but the rest are in a better case; they know more than when they were children, they understand better, their desires and sympathies answer more nimbly to the provocation of the senses, and their minds are brimming with interest as they go about the world.

According to my contention, this is a flight to which children cannot rise. They are wheeled in perambulators or dragged about by nurses in a pleasing stupor. A vague, faint, abiding wonderment possesses them. Here and there some specially remarkable circumstance, such as a water-cart or a guardsman, fairly penetrates into the seat of thought and calls them, for half a moment, out of themselves; and you may see them, still towed forward sideways by the inexorable nurse as by a sort of destiny, but still staring at the bright object in their wake. It may be some minutes before another such moving spectacle reawakens them to the world in which they dwell. For other children, they almost invariably show some intelligent sympathy. "There is a fine fellow making mud pies," they seem to say; "that I can understand, there is some sense in mud pies." But the doings of their elders, unless where they are speakingly picturesque or recommend themselves by the quality of being easily imitable, they let them go over their heads (as we say) without the least regard. If it were not for this perpetual imitation, we should be tempted to fancy they despised us outright, or only considered us in the light of creatures brutally strong and brutally silly; among whom they condescended to dwell in obedience like a philosopher at a barbarous court. At times, indeed, they display an arrogance of disregard that is truly staggering. Once, when I was groaning aloud with physical pain, a young gentleman came into the room and nonchalantly inquired if I had seen his bow and arrow. He made no account of my groans, which he accepted, as he had to accept so much else, as a piece of the inexplicable conduct of his elders; and like a wise young gentleman, he would waste no wonder on the subject. Those elders, who care so little for rational enjoyment, and are even the enemies of rational enjoyment for others, he had accepted without understanding and without complaint, as the rest of us accept the scheme of the universe.

We grown people can tell ourselves a story, give and take strokes until the bucklers ring, ride far and fast, marry, fall, and die; all the while sitting quietly by the fire or lying prone in bed. This is exactly what a child cannot do, or does not do, at least, when he can find anything else. He works all with lay figures and stage properties. When his story comes to the fighting, he must rise, get something by way of a sword and have a set-to with a piece of furniture, until he is out of breath. When he comes to ride with the king's pardon, he must bestride a chair, which he will so hurry and belabour and on which he will so furiously demean himself, that the messenger will arrive, if not bloody with spurring, at least fiery red with haste. If his romance involves an accident upon a cliff, he must clamber in person about the chest of drawers and fall bodily upon the carpet, before his imagination is satisfied. Lead soldiers, dolls, all toys, in short, are in the same category and answer the same end. Nothing can stagger a child's faith; he accepts the clumsiest substitutes and can swallow the most staring incongruities. The chair he has just been besieging as a castle, or valiantly cutting to the ground as a dragon, is taken away for the accommodation of a morning visitor, and he is nothing abashed; he can skirmish by the hour with a stationary coal-scuttle; in the midst of the enchanted pleasance, he can see, without sensible shock, the gardener soberly digging potatoes for the day's dinner. He can make abstraction of whatever does not fit into his fable; and he puts his eyes into his pocket, just as we hold our noses in an unsavoury lane. And so it is, that although the ways of children cross with those of their elders in a hundred places daily, they never go in the same direction nor so much as lie in the same element. So may the telegraph wires intersect the line of the highroad, or so might a landscape painter and a bagman visit the same country, and yet move in different worlds.

People struck with these spectacles cry aloud about the power of imagination in the young. Indeed there may be two words to that. It is, in some ways, but a pedestrian fancy that the child exhibits. It is the grown people who make the nursery stories; all the children do, is jealously to preserve the text. One out of a dozen reasons why *Robinson Crusoe* should be so popular with youth, is that it hits their level in this matter to a nicety; Crusoe was always at makeshifts and had, in so many words, to *play* at a great variety of professions; and then the book is all about tools, and there is nothing that delights a child so much. Hammers and saws belong to a province of life that positively calls for imitation. The juvenile lyrical drama, surely of the most ancient Thespian model, wherein the trades of mankind are successively simulated to the running burthen "On a cold and frosty morning," gives a good instance of the artistic taste in children. And this need for overt action and lay figures testifies to a defect in the child's imagination which prevents him from carrying out his novels in the privacy of his own heart. He does not yet know enough of the world and men. His experience is incomplete. That stage-wardrobe and scene-room that we call the memory is so ill provided, that he can overtake few combinations and body out few stories, to his own content, without some external aid. He is at the experimental stage; he is not sure how one would feel in certain circumstances; to make sure, he must come as near trying it as his means permit. And so here is young heroism with a wooden sword, and mothers practise their kind vocation over a bit of jointed stick. It may be laughable enough just now; but it is these same people and these same thoughts, that not long hence, when they are on the theatre of life, will make you weep and tremble. For children think very much the same thoughts and dream the same dreams as bearded men and marriageable women. No one is more romantic. Fame and honour, the love of young men and the love of mothers, the business man's pleasure in method, all these and others they anticipate and rehearse in their play hours. Upon us, who are further advanced and fairly dealing with the threads of destiny, they only glance from time to time to glean a hint for their own mimetic reproduction. Two children playing at soldiers are far more interesting to each other than one of the scarlet beings whom both are busy imitating. This is perhaps the greatest oddity of all. "Art for art" is their motto; and the doings of grown folk are only interesting as the raw material for play. Not Théophile Gautier, not Flaubert, can look more callously upon life, or rate the reproduction more highly over the reality; and they will parody an execution, a deathbed, or the funeral of the young man of Nain, with all the cheerfulness in the world.

The true parallel for play is not to be found, of course, in conscious art, which, though it be derived from play, is itself an abstract, impersonal thing, and depends largely upon philosophical interests beyond the scope of childhood. It is when we make castles in the air and personate the leading character in our own romances, that we return to the spirit of our first years. Only, there are several reasons why the spirit is no longer so agreeable to indulge. Nowadays, when we admit this personal element into our divagations we are apt to stir up uncomfortable and sorrowful memories, and remind ourselves sharply of old wounds. Our day-dreams can no longer lie all in the air like a story in the *Arabian Nights;* they read to us rather like the history of a period in which we ourselves had taken part, where we come across many unfortunate passages and find our own conduct smartly reprimanded. And then the child, mind you, acts his parts. He does not merely repeat them to himself; he leaps, he runs, and sets the blood agog over all his body. And so his play breathes him; and he no sooner assumes a passion than he gives it vent. Alas! when we betake ourselves to our intellectual form of play, sitting quietly by the fire or lying prone in bed, we rouse many hot feelings for which we can find no outlet. Substitutes are not acceptable to the mature mind, which desires the thing itself; and even to rehearse a triumphant dialogue with one's enemy, although it is perhaps the most satisfactory piece of play still left within our reach, is not entirely satisfying, and is even apt to lead to a visit and an interview which may be the reverse of triumphant after all.

In the child's world of dim sensation, play is all in all. "Making believe" is the gist of his whole life, and he cannot so much as take a walk except in character. I could not learn my alphabet without some suitable *mise-en-scène*, and had to act a business man in an office before I could sit down to my book. Will you kindly question your memory, and find out how much you did, work or pleasure, in good faith and soberness, and for how much you had to cheat yourself with some invention? I remember, as though it were yesterday, the expansion of spirit, the dignity and self-reliance, that came with a pair of mustachios in burnt cork, even when there was none to see. Children are even content to forego what we call the realities, and prefer the shadow to the substance. When they might be speaking intelligibly together, they chatter senseless gibberish by the hour, and are quite happy because they are making believe to speak French. I have said already how even the imperious appetite of hunger suffers itself to be gulled and led by the nose with the fag end of an old song. And it goes deeper than this: when children are together even a meal is felt as an interruption in the business of life; and they must find some imaginative sanction, and tell themselves some sort of story, to account for, to colour, to render entertaining, the simple processes of eating and drinking. What wonderful fancies I have heard evolved out of the pattern upon tea-cups!—from which there followed a code of rules and a whole world of excitement, until tea-drinking began to take rank as a game. When my cousin and I took our porridge of a morning, we had a device to enliven the course of the meal. He ate his with sugar, and explained it to be a country continually buried under snow. I took mine with milk, and explained it to be a country suffering gradual inundation. You can imagine us exchanging bulletins; how here was an island still unsubmerged, here a valley not yet covered with snow; what inventions were made; how his population lived in cabins on perches and travelled on stilts, and how mine was always in boats; how the interest grew furious, as the last corner of safe ground was cut off on all sides and grew smaller every moment; and how in fine, the food was of altogether secondary importance, and might even have been nauseous, so long as we seasoned it with these dreams. But perhaps the most exciting moments I ever had over a meal, were in the case of calves'-feet jelly. It was hardly possible not to believe—and you may be sure, so far from trying, I did all I could to favour the illusion—that some part of it was hollow, and that sooner or later my spoon would lay open the secret tabernacle of the golden rock. There, might some miniature *Red Beard* await his hour; there, might one find the treasures of the *Forty Thieves*, and bewildered Cassim beating about the walls. And so I quarried on slowly, with bated breath, savouring the interest. Believe me, I had little palate left for the jelly; and though I preferred the taste when I took cream with it, I used often to go without, because the cream dimmed the transparent fractures.

Even with games, this spirit is authoritative with right-minded children. It is thus that hide-and-seek has so pre-eminent a sovereignty, for it is the wellspring of romance, and the actions and the excitement to which it gives rise lend themselves to almost any sort of fable. And thus cricket, which is a mere matter of dexterity, palpably about nothing and for no end, often fails to satisfy infantile craving. It is a game, if you like, but not a game of play. You cannot tell yourself a story about cricket; and the activity it calls forth can be justified on no rational theory. Even football, although it admirably simulates the tug and the ebb and flow of battle, has presented difficulties to the mind of young sticklers after verisimilitude; and I knew at least one little boy who was mightily exercised about the presence of the ball, and had to spirit himself up, whenever he came to play, with an elaborate story of enchantment, and take the missile as a sort of talisman bandied about in conflict between two Arabian nations.

To think of such a frame of mind is to become disquieted about the bringing up of children. Surely they dwell in a mythological epoch, and are not the contemporaries of their parents. What can they think of them? what can they make of these bearded or petticoated giants who look down upon their games? who move upon a cloudy Olympus, following unknown designs apart from rational enjoyment? who profess the tenderest solicitude for children, and yet every now and again reach down out of their altitude and terribly vindicate the prerogatives of age? Off goes the child, corporally smarting, but morally rebellious. Were there ever such unthinkable deities as parents? I would give a great deal to know what, in nine cases out of ten, is the child's unvarnished feeling. A sense of past cajolery; a sense of personal attraction, at best very feeble; above all, I should imagine, a sense of terror for the untried residue of mankind: go to make up the attraction that he feels. No wonder, poor little heart, with such a weltering world in front of him, if he clings to the hand he knows! The dread irrationality of the whole affair, as it seems to children, is a thing we are all too ready to forget. "Oh, why," I remember passionately wondering, "why can we not all be happy and devote ourselves to play?" And when children do philosophise, I believe it is usually to very much the same purpose.

One thing, at least, comes very clearly out of these considerations; that whatever we are to expect at the hands of children, it should not be any peddling exactitude about matters of fact. They walk in a vain show, and among mists and rainbows; they are passionate after dreams and unconcerned about realities; speech is a difficult art not wholly learned; and there is nothing in their own tastes or purposes to teach them what we mean by abstract truthfulness. When a bad writer is inexact, even if he can look back on half a century of years, we charge him with incompetence and not with dishonesty. And why not extend the same allowance to imperfect speakers? Let a stockbroker be dead stupid about poetry, or a poet inexact in the details of business, and we excuse them heartily from blame. But show us a miserable, unbreeched, human entity, whose whole profession it is to take a tub for a fortified town and a shaving-brush for the deadly stiletto, and who passes three-fourths of his time in a dream and the rest in open self-deception, and we expect him to be as nice upon a matter of fact as a scientific expert bearing evidence. Upon my heart, I think it less than decent. You do not consider how little the child sees, or how swift he is to weave what he has seen into bewildering fiction; and that he cares no more for what you call truth, than you for a gingerbread dragoon.

I am reminded, as I write, that the child is very inquiring as to the precise truth of stories. But indeed this is a very different matter, and one bound up with the subject of play, and the precise amount of playfulness, or playability, to be looked for in the world. Many such burning questions must arise in the course of nursery education. Among the fauna of this planet, which already embraces the pretty soldier and the terrifying Irish beggar-man, is, or is not, the child to expect a Blue-beard or a Cormoran? Is he, or is he not, to look out for magicians, kindly and potent? May he, or may he not, reasonably hope to be cast away upon a desert island, or turned to such diminutive proportions that he can live on equal terms with his lead soldiery, and go a cruise in his own toy schooner? Surely all these are practical questions to a neophyte entering upon life with a view to play. Precision upon such a point, the child can understand. But if you merely ask him of his past behaviour, as to who threw such a stone, for instance, or struck such and such a match; or whether he had looked into a parcel or gone by a forbidden path,—why, he can see no moment in the inquiry, and it is ten to one, he has already half forgotten and half bemused himself with subsequent imaginings.

It would be easy to leave them in their native cloud-land, where they figure so prettily—pretty like flowers and innocent like dogs. They will come out of their gardens soon enough, and have to go into offices and the witness-box. Spare them yet a while, O conscientious parent! Let them doze among their playthings yet a little! for who knows what a rough, warfaring existence lies before them in the future?

# WALKING TOURS

# WALKING TOURS

It must not be imagined that a walking tour, as some would have us fancy, is merely a better or worse way of seeing the country. There are many ways of seeing landscape quite as good; and none more vivid, in spite of canting dilettantes, than from a railway train. But landscape on a walking tour is quite accessory. He who is indeed of the brotherhood does not voyage in quest of the picturesque, but of certain jolly humours—of the hope and spirit with which the march begins at morning, and the peace and spiritual repletion of the evening's rest. He cannot tell whether he puts his knapsack on, or takes it off, with more delight. The excitement of the departure puts him in key for that of the arrival. Whatever he does is not only a reward in itself, but will be further rewarded in the sequel; and so pleasure leads on to pleasure in an endless chain. It is this that so few can understand; they will either be always lounging or always at five miles an hour; they do not play off the one against the other, prepare all day for the evening, and all evening for the next day. And, above all, it is here that your overwalker fails of comprehension. His heart rises against those who drink their curaçoa in liqueur glasses, when he himself can swill it in a brown John. He will not believe that the flavour is more delicate in the smaller dose. He will not believe that to walk this unconscionable distance is merely to stupefy and brutalise himself, and come to his inn, at night, with a sort of frost on his five wits, and a starless night of darkness in his spirit. Not for him the mild luminous evening of the temperate walker! He has nothing left of man but a physical need for bedtime and a double nightcap; and even his pipe, if he be a smoker, will be savourless and disenchanted. It is the fate of such an one to take twice as much trouble as is needed to obtain happiness, and miss the happiness in the end; he is the man of the proverb, in short, who goes further and fares worse.

Now, to be properly enjoyed, a walking tour should be gone upon alone. If you go in a company, or even in pairs, it is no longer a walking tour in anything but name; it is something else and more in the nature of a picnic. A walking tour should be gone upon alone, because freedom is of the essence; because you should be able to stop and go on, and follow this way or that, as the freak takes you; and because you must have your own pace, and neither trot alongside a champion walker, nor mince in time with a girl. And then you must be open to all impressions and let your thoughts take colour from what you see. You should be as a pipe for any wind to play upon. "I cannot see the wit," says Hazlitt, "of walking and talking at the same time. When I am in the country I wish to vegetate like the country,"—which is the gist of all that can be said upon the matter. There should be no cackle of voices at your elbow, to jar on the meditative silence of the morning. And so long as a man is reasoning he cannot surrender himself to that fine intoxication that comes of much motion in the open air, that begins in a sort of dazzle and sluggishness of the brain, and ends in a peace that passes comprehension.

During the first day or so of any tour there are moments of bitterness, when the traveller feels more than coldly towards his knapsack, when he is half in a mind to throw it bodily over the hedge and, like Christian on a similar occasion, "give three leaps and go on singing." And yet it soon acquires a property of easiness. It becomes magnetic; the spirit of the journey enters into it. And no sooner have you passed the straps over your shoulder than the lees of sleep are cleared from you, you pull yourself together with a shake, and fall at once into your stride. And surely, of all possible moods, this, in which a man takes the road, is the best. Of course, if he *will* keep thinking of his anxieties, if he *will* open the merchant Abudah's chest and walk arm-in-arm with the hag—why, wherever he is, and whether he walk fast or slow, the chances are that he will not be happy. And so much the more shame to himself! There are perhaps thirty men setting forth at that same hour, and I would lay a large wager there is not another dull face among the thirty. It would be a fine thing to follow, in a coat of darkness, one after another of these wayfarers, some summer morning, for the first few miles upon the road. This one, who walks fast, with a keen look in his eyes, is all concentrated in his own mind; he is up at his loom, weaving and weaving, to set the landscape to words. This one peers about, as he goes, among the grasses; he waits by the canal to watch the dragon-flies; he leans on the gate of the pasture, and cannot look enough upon the complacent kine. And here comes another, talking, laughing, and gesticulating to himself. His face changes from time to time, as indignation flashes from his eyes or anger clouds his forehead. He is composing articles, delivering orations, and conducting the most impassioned interviews, by the way. A little farther on, and it is as like as not he will begin to sing. And well for him, supposing him to be no great master in that art, if he stumble across no stolid peasant at a corner; for on such an occasion, I scarcely know which is the more troubled, or whether it is worse to suffer the confusion of your troubadour, or the unfeigned alarm of your clown. A sedentary population, accustomed, besides, to the strange mechanical bearing of the common tramp, can in no wise explain to itself the gaiety of these passers-by. I knew one man who was arrested as a runaway lunatic, because although a full-grown person with a red beard, he skipped as he went like a child. And you would be astonished if I were to tell you all the grave and learned heads who have confessed to me that, when on walking tours, they sang—and sang very ill—and had a pair of red ears when, as described above, the inauspicious peasant plumped into their arms from round a corner. And here, lest you should think I am exaggerating, is Hazlitt's own confession, from his essay *On Going a Journey*, which is so good that there should be a tax levied on all who have not read it:—

"Give me the clear blue sky over my head," says he, "and the green turf beneath my feet, a winding road before me, and a three hours' march to dinner—and then to thinking! It is hard if I cannot start some game on these lone heaths. I laugh, I run, I leap, I sing for joy."

Bravo! After that adventure of my friend with the policeman, you would not have cared, would you, to publish that in the first person? But we have no bravery nowadays, and, even in books, must all pretend to be as dull and foolish as our neighbours. It was not so with Hazlitt. And notice how learned he is (as, indeed, throughout the essay) in the theory of walking tours. He is none of your athletic men in purple stockings, who walk their fifty miles a day: three hours' march is his ideal. And then he must have a winding road, the epicure!

Yet there is one thing I object to in these words of his, one thing in the great master's practice that seems to me not wholly wise. I do not approve of that leaping and running. Both of these hurry the respiration; they both shake up the brain out of its glorious open-air confusion; and they both break the pace. Uneven walking is not so agreeable to the body, and it distracts and irritates the mind. Whereas, when once you have fallen into an equable stride, it requires no conscious thought from you to keep it up, and yet it prevents you from thinking earnestly of anything else. Like knitting, like the work of a copying clerk, it gradually neutralises and sets to sleep the serious activity of the mind. We can think of this or that, lightly and laughingly, as a child thinks, or as we think in a morning doze; we can make puns or puzzle out acrostics, and trifle in a thousand ways with words and rhymes; but when it comes to honest work, when we come to gather ourselves together for an effort, we may sound the trumpet as loud and long as we please; the great barons of the mind will not rally to the standard, but sit, each one, at home, warming his hands over his own fire and brooding on his own private thought!

In the course of a day's walk, you see, there is much variance in the mood. From the exhilaration of the start, to the happy phlegm of the arrival, the change is certainly great. As the day goes on, the traveller moves from the one extreme towards the other. He becomes more and more incorporated with the material landscape, and the open-air drunkenness grows upon him with great strides, until he posts along the road, and sees everything about him, as in a cheerful dream. The first is certainly brighter, but the second stage is the more peaceful. A man does not make so many articles towards the end, nor does he laugh aloud; but the purely animal pleasures, the sense of physical wellbeing, the delight of every inhalation, of every time the muscles tighten down the thigh, console him for the absence of the others, and bring him to his destination still content.

Nor must I forget to say a word on bivouacs. You come to a milestone on a hill, or some place where deep ways meet under trees; and off goes the knapsack, and down you sit to smoke a pipe in the shade. You sink into yourself, and the birds come round and look at you; and your smoke dissipates upon the afternoon under the blue dome of heaven; and the sun lies warm upon your feet, and the cool air visits your neck and turns aside your open shirt. If you are not happy, you must have an evil conscience. You may dally as long as you like by the roadside. It is almost as if the millennium were arrived, when we shall throw our clocks and watches over the housetop, and remember time and seasons no more. Nor to keep hours for a lifetime is, I was going to say, to live for ever. You have no idea, unless you have tried it, how endlessly long is a summer's day, that you measure out only by hunger, and bring to an end only when you are drowsy. I know a village where there are hardly any clocks, where no one knows more of the days of the week than by a sort of instinct for the fête on Sundays, and where only one person can tell you the day of the month, and she is generally wrong; and if people were aware how slow Time journeyed in that village, and what armfuls of spare hours he gives, over and above the bargain, to its wise inhabitants, I believe there would be a stampede out of London, Liverpool, Paris, and a variety of large towns, where the clocks lose their heads, and shake the hours out each one faster than the other, as though they were all in a wager. And all these foolish pilgrims would each bring his own misery along with him, in a watch-pocket! It is to be noticed, there were no clocks and watches in the much-vaunted days before the flood. It follows, of course, there were no appointments, and punctuality was not yet thought upon. "Though ye take from a covetous man all his treasure," says Milton, "he has yet one jewel left; ye cannot deprive him of his covetousness." And so I would say of a modern man of business, you may do what you will for him, put him in Eden, give him the elixir of life—he has still a flaw at heart, he still has his business habits. Now, there is no time when business habits are more mitigated than on a walking tour. And so during these halts, as I say, you will feel almost free.

But it is at night, and after dinner, that the best hour comes. There are no such pipes to be smoked as those that follow a good day's march; the flavour of the tobacco is a thing to be remembered, it is so dry and aromatic, so full and so fine. If you wind up the evening with grog, you will own there was never such grog; at every sip a jocund tranquillity spreads about your limbs, and sits easily in your heart. If you read a book—and you will never do so save by fits and starts—you find the language strangely racy and harmonious; words take a new meaning; single sentences possess the ear for half-an-hour together; and the writer endears himself to you, at every page, by the nicest coincidence of sentiment. It seems as if it were a book you had written yourself in a dream. To all we have read on such occasions we look back with special favour. "It was on the 10th of April, 1798," says Hazlitt, with amorous precision, "that I sat down to a volume of the new *Héloïse*, at the Inn at Llangollen, over a bottle of sherry and a cold chicken." I should wish to quote more, for though we are mighty fine fellows nowadays, we cannot write like Hazlitt. And, talking of that, a volume of Hazlitt's essays would be a capital pocket-book on such a journey; so would a volume of Heine's songs; and for *Tristram Shandy* I can pledge a fair experience.

If the evening be fine and warm, there is nothing better in life than to lounge before the inn door in the sunset, or lean over the parapet of the bridge, to watch the weeds and the quick fishes. It is then, if ever, that you taste Joviality to the full significance of that audacious word. Your muscles are so agreeably slack, you feel so clean and so strong and so idle, that whether you move or sit still, whatever you do is done with pride and a kingly sort of pleasure. You fall in talk with any one, wise or foolish, drunk or sober. And it seems as if a hot walk purged you, more than of anything else, of all narrowness and pride, and left curiosity to play its part freely, as in a child or a man of science. You lay aside all your own hobbies, to watch provincial humours develop themselves before you, now as a laughable farce, and now grave and beautiful like an old tale.

Or perhaps you are left to your own company for the night, and surly weather imprisons you by the fire. You may remember how Burns, numbering past pleasures, dwells upon the hours when he has been "happy thinking." It is a phrase that may well perplex a poor modern, girt about on every side by clocks and chimes, and haunted, even at night, by flaming dial-plates. For we are all so busy, and have so many far-off projects to realise, and castles in the fire to turn into solid habitable mansions on a gravel soil, that we can find no time for pleasure trips into the Land of Thought and among the Hills of Vanity. Changed times, indeed, when we must sit all night, beside the fire, with folded hands; and a changed world for most of us, when we find we can pass the hours without discontent, and be happy thinking. We are in such haste to be doing, to be writing, to be gathering gear, to make our voice audible a moment in the derisive silence of eternity, that we forget that one thing, of which these are but the parts—namely, to live. We fall in love, we drink hard, we run to and fro upon the earth like frightened sheep. And now you are to ask yourself if, when all is done, you would not have been better to sit by the fire at home and be happy thinking. To sit still and contemplate,—to remember the faces of women without desire, to be pleased by the great deeds of men without envy, to be everything and everywhere in sympathy, and yet content to remain where and what you are—is not this to know both wisdom and virtue, and to dwell with happiness? After all, it is not they who carry flags, but they who look upon it from a private chamber, who have the fun of the procession. And once you are at that, you are in the very humour of all social heresy. It is no time for shuffling, or for big, empty words. If you ask yourself what you mean by fame, riches, or learning, the answer is far to seek; and you go back into that kingdom of light imaginations, which seem so vain in the eyes of Philistines perspiring after wealth, and so momentous to those who are stricken with the disproportions of the world, and, in the face of the gigantic stars, cannot stop to split differences between two degrees of the infinitesimally small, such as a tobacco-pipe or the Roman Empire, a million of money or a fiddlestick's end.

You lean from the window, your last pipe reeking whitely into the darkness, your body full of delicious pains, your mind enthroned in the seventh circle of content; when suddenly the mood changes, the weather-cock goes about, and you ask yourself one question more: whether, for the interval, you have been the wisest philosopher or the most egregious of donkeys? Human experience is not yet able to reply; but at least you have had a fine moment, and looked down upon all the kingdoms of the earth. And whether it was wise or foolish, to-morrow's travel will carry you, body and mind, into some different parish of the infinite.

# PAN'S PIPES

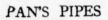

# PAN'S PIPES

The world in which we live has been variously said and sung by the most ingenious poets and philosophers: these reducing it to formulæ and chemical ingredients, those striking the lyre in high-sounding measures for the handiwork of God. What experience supplies is of a mingled tissue, and the choosing mind has much to reject before it can get together the materials of a theory. Dew and thunder, destroying Atilla and the Spring lambkins, belong to an order of contrasts which no repetition can assimilate. There is an uncouth, outlandish strain throughout the web of the world, as from a vexatious planet in the house of life. Things are not congruous and wear strange disguises: the consummate flower is fostered out of dung, and after nourishing itself awhile with heaven's delicate distillations, decays again into indistinguishable soil; and with Cæsar's ashes, Hamlet tells us, the urchins make dirt pies and filthily besmear their countenances. Nay, the kindly shine of summer, when tracked home with the scientific spy-glass, is found to issue from the most portentous nightmare of the universe—the great, conflagrant sun: a world of hell's squibs, tumultuary, roaring aloud, inimical to life. The sun itself is enough to disgust a human being of the scene which he inhabits; and you would not fancy there was a green or habitable spot in a universe thus awfully lighted up.

And yet it is by the blaze of such a conflagration, to which the fire of Rome was but a spark, that we do all our fiddling, and hold domestic tea-parties at the arbour door.

The Greeks figured Pan, the god of Nature, now terribly stamping his foot, so that armies were dispersed; now by the woodside on a summer noon trolling on his pipe until he charmed the hearts of upland ploughmen. And the Greeks, in so figuring, uttered the last word of human experience. To certain smoke-dried spirits matter and motion and elastic æthers, and the hypothesis of this or that other spectacled professor, tell a speaking story; but for youth and all ductile and congenial minds, Pan is not dead, but of all the classic hierarchy alone survives in triumph; goat-footed, with a gleeful and an angry look, the type of the shaggy world: and in every wood, if you go with a spirit properly prepared, you shall hear the note of his pipe.

For it is a shaggy world, and yet studded with gardens; where the salt and tumbling sea receives clear rivers running from among reeds and lilies; fruitful and austere; a rustic world; sunshiny, lewd, and cruel. What is it the birds sing among the trees in pairing-time? What means the sound of the rain falling far and wide upon the leafy forest? To what tune does the fisherman whistle, as he hauls in his net at morning, and the bright fish are heaped inside the boat? These are all airs upon Pan's pipe; he it was who gave them breath in the exultation of his heart, and gleefully modulated their outflow with his lips and fingers. The coarse mirth of herdsmen, shaking the dells with laughter and striking out high echoes from the rock; the tune of moving feet in the lamplit city, or on the smooth ballroom floor; the hooves of many horses, beating the wide pastures in alarm; the song of hurrying rivers; the colour of clear skies; and smiles and the live touch of hands; and the voice of things, and their significant look, and the renovating influence they breathe forth—these are his joyful measures, to which the whole earth treads in choral harmony. To this music the young lambs bound as to a tabor, and the London shop-girl skips rudely in the dance. For it puts a spirit of gladness in all hearts; and to look on the happy side of nature is common, in their hours, to all created things. Some are vocal under a good influence, are pleasing whenever they are pleased, and hand on their happiness to others, as a child who, looking upon lovely things, looks lovely. Some leap to the strains with unapt foot, and make a halting figure in the universal dance. And some, like sour spectators at the play, receive the music into their hearts with an unmoved countenance, and walk like strangers through the general rejoicing. But let him feign never so carefully, there is not a man but has his pulses shaken when Pan trolls out a stave of ecstasy and sets the world a-singing.

Alas if that were all! But oftentimes the air is changed; and in the screech of the night wind, chasing navies, subverting the tall ships and the rooted cedar of the hills; in the random deadly levin or the fury of headlong floods, we recognise the "dread foundation" of life and the anger in Pan's heart. Earth wages open war against her children, and under her softest touch hides treacherous claws. The cool waters invite us in to drown; the domestic hearth burns up in the hour of sleep, and makes an end of all. Everything is good or bad, helpful or deadly, not in itself, but by its circumstances. For a few bright days in England the hurricane must break forth and the North Sea pay a toll of populous ships. And when the universal music has led lovers into the path of dalliance, confident of Nature's sympathy, suddenly the air shifts into a minor, and death makes a clutch from his ambuscade below the bed of marriage. For death is given a kiss; the dearest kindnesses are fatal; and into this life, where one thing preys upon another, the child too often makes its entrance from the mother's corpse. It is no wonder, with so traitorous a scheme of things, if the wise people who created for us the idea of Pan thought that of all fears the fear of him was the most terrible, since it embraces all. And still we preserve the phrase: a panic terror. To reckon dangers too curiously, to hearken too intently for the threat that runs through all the winning music of the world, to hold back the hand from the rose because of the thorn, and from life because of death: this it is to be afraid of Pan. Highly respectable citizens who flee life's pleasures and responsibilities and keep, with upright hat, upon the midway of custom, avoiding the right hand and the left, the ecstasies and the agonies, how surprised they would be if they could hear their attitude mythologically expressed, and knew themselves as tooth-chattering ones, who flee from Nature because they fear the hand of Nature's God! Shrilly sound Pan's pipes; and behold the banker instantly concealed in the bank parlour! For to distrust one's impulses is to be recreant to Pan.

There are moments when the mind refuses to be satisfied with evolution, and demands a ruddier presentation of the sum of man's experience. Sometimes the mood is brought about by laughter at the humorous side of life, as when, abstracting ourselves from earth, we imagine people plodding on foot, or seated in ships and speedy trains, with the planet all the while whirling in the opposite direction, so that, for all their hurry, they travel back-foremost through the universe of space. Sometimes it comes by the spirit of delight, and sometimes by the spirit of terror. At least, there will always be hours when we refuse to be put off by the feint of explanation, nicknamed science; and demand instead some palpitating image of our estate, that shall represent the troubled and uncertain element in which we dwell, and satisfy reason by the means of art. Science writes of the world as if with the cold finger of a starfish; it is all true; but what is it when compared to the reality of which it discourses? where hearts beat high in April, and death strikes, and hills totter in the earthquake, and there is a glamour over all the objects of sight, and a thrill in all noises for the ear, and Romance herself has made her dwelling among men? So we come back to the old myth, and hear the goat-footed piper making the music which is itself the charm and terror of things; and when a glen invites our visiting footsteps, fancy that Pan leads us thither with a gracious tremolo; or when our hearts quail at the thunder of the cataract, tell ourselves that he has stamped his hoof in the nigh thicket.

# A PLEA FOR GAS LAMPS

# A PLEA FOR GAS LAMPS

CITIES given, the problem was to light them. How to conduct individual citizens about the burgess-warren, when once heaven had withdrawn its leading luminary? or—since we live in a scientific age—when once our spinning planet has turned its back upon the sun? The moon, from time to time, was doubtless very helpful; the stars had a cheery look among the chimney-pots; and a cresset here and there, on church or citadel, produced a fine pictorial effect, and, in places where the ground lay unevenly, held out the right hand of conduct to the benighted. But sun, moon, and stars abstracted or concealed, the night-faring inhabitant had to fall back—we speak on the authority of old prints—upon stable lanthorns two storeys in height. Many holes, drilled in the conical turret-roof of this vagabond Pharos, let up spouts of dazzlement into the bearer's eyes; and as he paced forth in the ghostly darkness, carrying his own sun by a ring about his finger, day and night swung to and fro and up and down about his footsteps. Blackness haunted his path; he was beleagured by goblins as he went; and, curfew being struck, he found no light but that he travelled in throughout the township.

Closely following on this epoch of migratory lanthorns in a world of extinction, came the era of oil-lights, hard to kindle, easy to extinguish, pale and wavering in the hour of their endurance. Rudely puffed the winds of heaven; roguishly clomb up the all-destructive urchin; and, lo! in a moment night re-established her void empire, and the cit groped along the wall, suppered but bedless, occult from guidance, and sorrily wading in the kennels. As if gamesome winds and gamesome youths were not sufficient, it was the habit to sling these fable luminaries from house to house above the fairway. There, on invisible cordage, let them swing! And suppose some crane-necked general to go speeding by on a tall charger, spurring the destiny of nations, red-hot in expedition, there would indubitably be some effusion of military blood, and oaths, and a certain crash of glass; and while the chieftain rode forward with a purple coxcomb, the street would be left to original darkness, unpiloted, unvoyageable, a province of the desert night.

The conservative, looking before and after, draws from each contemplation the matter for content. Out of the age of gas lamps he glances back slightingly at the mirk and glimmer in which his ancestors wandered; his heart waxes jocund at the contrast; nor do his lips refrain from a stave, in the highest style of poetry, lauding progress and the golden mean. When gas first spread along a city, mapping it forth about evenfall for the eye of observant birds, a new age had begun for sociality and corporate pleasure-seeking, and begun with proper circumstance, becoming its own birthright. The work of Prometheus had advanced by another stride. Mankind and its supper parties were no longer at the mercy of a few miles of sea-fog; sundown no longer emptied the promenade; and the day was lengthened out to every man's fancy. The city-folk had stars of their own; biddable, domesticated stars.

It is true that these were not so steady, nor yet so clear, as their originals; nor indeed was their lustre so elegant as that of the best wax candles. But then the gas stars, being nearer at hand, were more practically efficacious than Jupiter himself. It is true, again, that they did not unfold their rays with the appropriate spontaneity of the planets, coming out along the firmament one after another, as the need arises. But the lamplighters took to their heels every evening, and ran with a good heart. It was pretty to see man thus emulating the punctuality of heaven's orbs; and though perfection was not absolutely reached, and now and then an individual may have been knocked on the head by the ladder of the flying functionary, yet people commended his zeal in a proverb, and taught their children to say, "God bless the lamplighter!" And since his passage was a piece of the day's programme, the children were well pleased to repeat the benediction, not, of course, in so many words, which would have been improper, but in some chaste circumlocution, suitable for infant lips.

God bless him, indeed! For the term of his twilight diligence is near at hand; and for not much longer shall we watch him speeding up the street and, at measured intervals, knocking another luminous hole into the dusk. The Greeks would have made a noble myth of such an one; how he distributed starlight, and, as soon as the need was over, re-collected it; and the little bull's-eye, which was his instrument, and held enough fire to kindle a whole parish, would have been fitly commemorated in the legend. Now, like all heroic tasks, his labours draw towards apotheosis, and in the light of victory himself shall disappear. For another advance has been effected. Our tame stars are to come out in future, not one by one, but all in a body and at once. A sedate electrician somewhere in a back office touches a spring—and behold! from one end to another of the city, from east to west, from the Alexandra to the Crystal Palace, there is light! *Fiat Lux*, says the sedate electrician. What a spectacle, on some clear, dark nightfall, from the edge of Hampstead Hill, when in a moment, in the twinkling of an eye, the design of the monstrous city flashes into vision—a glittering hieroglyph many square miles in extent; and when, to borrow and debase an image, all the evening street lamps burst together into song! Such is the spectacle of the future, preluded the other day by the experiment in Pall Mall. Star-rise by electricity, the most romantic flight of civilisation; the compensatory benefit for an innumerable array of factories and bankers' clerks. To the artistic spirit exercised about Thirlmere, here is a crumb of consolation; consolatory, at least, to such of them as look out upon the world through seeing eyes, and contentedly accept beauty where it comes.

But the conservative, while lauding progress, is ever timid of innovation; his is the hand upheld to counsel pause; his is the signal advising slow advance. The word *electricity* now sounds the note of danger. In Paris, at the mouth of the Passage des Princes, in the place before the Opera portico, and in the Rue Drouot at the *Figaro* office, a new sort of urban star now shines out nightly, horrible, unearthly, obnoxious to the human eye; a lamp for a nightmare! Such a light as this should shine only on murders and public crime, or along the corridors of lunatic asylums, a horror to heighten horror. To look at it only once is to fall in love with gas, which gives a warm domestic radiance fit to eat by. Mankind, you would have thought, might have remained content with what Prometheus stole for them and not gone fishing the profound heaven with kites to catch and domesticate the wildfire of the storm. Yet here we have the levin brand at our doors, and it is proposed that we should henceforward take our walks abroad in the glare of permanent lightning. A man need not be very superstitious if he scruple to follow his pleasures by the light of the Terror that Flieth, nor very epicurean if he prefer to see the face of beauty more becomingly displayed. That ugly blinding glare may not improperly advertise the home of slanderous *Figaro*, which is a back-shop to the infernal regions; but where soft joys prevail, where people are convoked to pleasure and the philosopher looks on smiling and silent, where love and laughter and deifying wine abound, there, at least, let the old mild lustre shine upon the ways of man.

THE END

Printed by Spottiswoode, Ballantyne & Co. Ltd.
Colchester, London & Eton, England

C W